# THE IDEA BOOK

## 4TH AND 5TH GRADE

COOK MINISTRY RESOURCES

*a division of Cook Communications Ministries*
*4050 Lee Vance View, Colorado Springs, CO 80918-7100*
*Colorado Springs, Colorado/Paris, Ontario*

# TABLE OF CONTENTS

The Idea Book
Great Idea after Great Idea
after Great Idea
Cook Communications
Ministries
Colorado Springs,
Colorado/Paris, Ontario
© 1997 David C. Cook
Publishing Co.

Published by Cook Ministry
Resources
a division of Cook
Communications Ministries
4050 Lee Vance View,
Colorado Springs, CO 80918
Cable address: DCCOOK
First Printing, 1987
Printed in the United States of
America

Ideas on pages 6, 38, and 71-
73 are from *62 Activities for
Kids*, by Marlene LeFever,
© 1984, David C. Cook
Publishing Co.

The materials on pages 14, 27,
41, and 44 are from *Parade of
Plays*, a three book series by
David C. Cook Publishing Co.

Ideas on pages 8, 12, and 39
are from *Leader's Ideabank*,
David C. Cook Publishing Co.

**Contributors:**
Neta Jackson
Kathy Johnson
Sandy Karls
Robert Klausmeier
Marlene LeFever
Kathy Lewis
Eric Potter
Lucy Townsend

**Project Editor**
Lucy Townsend

**Editors:**
Matthew Eckmann
Kathy Lewis
Scottie May
Eric Potter

**Designer:**
Catherine Colten

**Illustrators:**
Andre Le Blanc
Susan Lexa
Johann Schumacher
Chris Sharp
Kathleen Weyna

# INTRODUCTION

What is your most vivid memory of children's church or Sunday school?

Ask adults this question, and many will recall the big events—times when they invested a lot of themselves in a Sunday school project. Maybe they dressed up in Bible-time costumes and put on a musical play for the congregation. Maybe they planned and put on an all-afternoon missionary fair. Or they might have constructed a Jerusalem marketplace and invited people from a nursing home to visit.

Some kids learn best when the usual classroom routine is set aside for a project that requires large-scale planning and creativity.

This book is designed for those kids. It is full of peak-experience activities that sometimes require lots of time and effort. In addition, it includes short projects that take only a few minutes.

Use this resource to involve the children who don't seem excited about church. Use it when you feel like doing something different.

Get set to make memories! ■

# I.
# YEARLONG PROJECTS

# WORSHIP JOURNEY
# NOTEBOOK

One good way for kids to recall their learning experiences is to keep a yearlong notebook.

The entire class might keep one worship notebook, or each student could keep his or her own notebook.

### The Cover

Students should cut a piece of construction paper the same size as the front of a notebook, and paste it in place.

Next they should draw one of their initials on heavy paper or cardboard and cut it out to use as a pattern.

The initial pattern should be traced several times on their construction paper until they have traced an interesting design. Consider overlapping the letters like the "G" in the sample.

Finally the children may color their design with bright crayons.

### The Inside of the Notebook

Throughout this yearlong study on worship, your students will be able to collect worship helps in their notebooks. You may want them to divide their notebooks into seven sections and label them like this:

Section 1—Things I want to thank God for.

Section 2—Prayers I would like God to answer.

Section 3—Prayers God has answered for me.

Section 4—My favorite worship hymns.

Section 5—My written prayers to God.

Section 6—My favorite Bible verses.

Section 7—My worship leadership roles.

The students will want to add to their notebooks as the year goes by. Encourage them to keep their notebooks up-to-date by writing in them at least once a week. ■

—ML

**THINGS YOU'LL NEED:**

- [ ] **notebooks, one for each child**
- [ ] **construction paper**
- [ ] **cardboard (or heavy paper)**
- [ ] **crayons/markers**

# Old Testament
## PICTURE TIME LINE

**THINGS
YOU'LL
NEED:**

- ☐ butcher paper
- ☐ felt-tipped markers/pencils
- ☐ *The Picture Bible*
- ☐ double-sided tape

**OPTIONAL:**

- ☐ opaque projector or photocopy machine
- ☐ scissors

This yearlong project will remind kids of the Old Testament chronology that they have learned this year in worship.

At the close of each unit, spread out a sheet of butcher paper at least two feet high and several feet long. There are two ways to picture key events and characters of the Bible stories from the unit just covered.

Have the children draw pictures depicting main events and characters in the order that they appear in *The Picture Bible*.

If you have an opaque projector or photocopy machine, you might enlarge pictures in *The Picture Bible*. Have kids color and attach them to the butcher paper. Underneath, they can print a title explaining the event.

As each unit's segment of the time line is completed, add it to the others on a classroom wall. By the end of the year, the Bible time line will probably stretch around all the walls of your classroom. A quick glance will show the students how far they have come in their study of the Old Testament. ■

# START A
# CHILDREN'S

**THINGS
YOU'LL
NEED:**
- [ ] **choir director**
- [ ] **kids who love to sing**
- [ ] **accompanist**

**by Julie Schmitz**

When you were a kid, did you take piano lessons (even if it was your mother's idea), or sing in a school choir, or play in the band? If not, do you wish you could have?

If you said yes, you probably would like your children to have the same opportunities. But many schools today aren't able to fund adequate music programs. If this is true in your case, must your children miss out?

No! The solution to this dilemma can be simple. A musical experience for your children is possible through the formation of their own church choir.

**Huddle: Plan Your Information**

Cultivate interest by talking with parents and children in your church family. Next, form a special committee to lay the foundation. Find someone willing to take on the job of director and children who wish to participate. Then build strong support from your church leaders and parents whose children will be involved.

For the director, choose an adult who can read music, carry a tune accurately, and produce a pleasant tone. A beautiful singing voice is not necessary, but the person should understand vocal production well enough to illustrate it and develop it in children. That person should

display a genuine fondness for children and be enthusiastic about the choir program. (If you need suggestions, the adult choir director may know just the right person to recruit.)

A big plus for any director is to have the help of a capable accompanist. Try to find another adult or a teenager who might be willing to do this.

**Pregame Strategy**

Here are some ways you, the committee, or your choir director can let church members know that a children's choir is being formed.

1. Ask someone good at designing posters to organize a poster campaign. Over a period of weeks prior to the first rehearsal, display a series of them that will build curiosity by giving information in bits and pieces. Post them in the most visible places around church. (Be sure the final one gives all the facts.)

2. Put to use the built-in means of publicizing events your church already has, such as bulletins and newsletters.

3. Mail letters to all potential choir members and their parents. Outline the program and stress its benefits.

4. Visit the Sunday school classrooms of the children who may join.

5. Telephone children to extend personal invitations.

6. If the choir is to begin in September, a good way to discover potential members is to include special music in the Vacation Bible School program. (Most courses include music relating to the theme, and some even have sing-along records.) The music leader could scout out those children who especially enjoy the music session. Then ask them to join the choir.

# CHURCH CHOIR

### Sizing Up Your Team

The size of your church and the number of interested children are the two main factors to consider when deciding which ages will comprise the choir. Are there enough to make up more than one? Then consider whether the director will lead more than one choir. More than likely, you'll only begin with one, but as your music program becomes more established, you'll have to expand.

| Preferred: | Possible |
| --- | --- |
| grades 1-3 | grades 1-6 |
| grades 4-6 | grades 2-6 |
| grades 7-8 | grades 3-8 |

Groups large enough to produce a good musical sound, but small enough to be easily managed are ideal.

### In-training Rules

The director and/or committee should set guidelines for the children and make them known from the very first rehearsal. (You might post them in the choir room, as well as supplying handouts for the children and parents.) Here are some positive actions choir members can demonstrate.

• Arrive a few minutes before the rehearsal to gather supplies and take seats.

• Participate in rehearsals and performances faithfully.

• Respect all music books, hymnals, Bibles, etc.

• Follow directions and behave appropriately during rehearsals.

• Strive toward musical growth by acquiring proper singing habits and increasing knowledge of fundamentals.

• Exhibit signs of spiritual growth, while learning that music allows everyone to worship God more effectively and provides a way to share a God-given gift with others.

### Uniforms for the Team

Even if you're stuck using old choir robes, you can achieve a new look by doing something as simple as adding bows to them. We did just that at our

church. And as a result, the bright red bows created a fresh appearance and "tied" the choir together as a group.

Or choose attire that most children already own: a white blouse or shirt, and a dark skirt or pair of slacks.

### Build Team Spirit

Provide opportunities for your choir members to get to know each other *and* you outside the walls of the choir room. Here are some ideas:

1. Decorate the walls of the rehearsal room with banners you've created together. (Use verses of Scripture relating to music for themes.)

2. Now and then, eat a meal together. Children can bring a sack lunch, while you supply the beverages. Follow this with games. Let the older children plan them if you wish.

3. Celebrate birthdays once a month for those sharing the same birth month. Arrange for the choir members' families to take turns supplying simple refreshments.

4. Attend a choral concert as a group. (This could be opened to families, too.)

5. Perform a service project for your church.

### Replay

To prove musical progress, tape the various stages of learning a song from the very beginning to the polished form. Then play the tape for the children so they can hear what they've accomplished. This will reinforce your verbal comments regarding their improvement.

### Challenge Your Team

Why not vary the types of musical accompaniment you use with your choir? Use records, background tapes or instrumentalists available in your church family. Invite Jim, a guitarist, or Tom, a trumpeter, to play with your choir.

It's also fun and educational for the children to perform an occasional anthem with the adult choir.

These extra efforts on your part will make the choir feel special.

### Extra Points

Provide encouragement to those children who are studying music privately. Why not set aside a small amount of time during one rehearsal a month to provide a built-in audience for ones who would like to perform? If Joyce says no to your first invitation, accept her answer cheerfully, but let her know she'll get another opportunity later. She may change her mind.

### Touchdown!

"Sometimes be sharp; never be flat; always be natural," is the saying on a plaque I spotted recently. How true! Children can tell when someone is being genuine. Be firm, but kind, consistent, encouraging, fair, loving supportive, and provide a good example. Enjoy each child and his or her natural gift of enthusiasm, maintain a sense of humor, and have fun! So, come on! Plan your strategy carefully to score that touchdown! ■

# Musical Instruments

Fourth and fifth grade kids usually love it when their parents are involved in their learning experiences. Enlist a parent who enjoys carpentry to help kids make musical instruments. Or help kids make these instruments yourself.

## Shakers

Have kids punch holes in the middle of the bottle caps with a hammer and large nail. Thread bottle caps on each of the 2 1/2" nails. Stain wood with brown shoe polish, and allow to dry. Have kids decide which end of the wood should be the handle. Then hammer the nails with the bottle caps in to the other end of the wood at 2" intervals.

Shakers can be beaten against the palm of the free hand or against other body parts.

## Cymbals

Punch a hole in the center of each pie pan. Stain the wooden drawer knobs with brown shoe polish and allow it to dry. Screw knobs into pie pans with a screwdriver.

Cymbals can be banged together for a loud sound. They can be brushed together for a soft sound.

## Drum

Cut construction paper to fit around the oatmeal container. Then decorate the paper with markers and fabric trims. After the construction paper decorations are dry, glue or tape construction paper to container. Now the drum is ready to be played. ■

**THINGS YOU'LL NEED TO MAKE SHAKERS:**
- [ ] 1" x 2" x 10" pieces of wood
- [ ] bottle caps
- [ ] One 5" nail
- [ ] 2 1/2" nails
- [ ] hammer
- [ ] brown shoe polish (or other stain)

**THINGS YOU'LL NEED TO MAKE CYMBALS:**
- [ ] aluminum pie pans
- [ ] wooden drawer knobs and 1/2" screws
- [ ] hammer
- [ ] nail
- [ ] screwdriver

**THINGS YOU'LL NEED TO MAKE A DRUM:**
- [ ] round oatmeal container
- [ ] light-colored construction paper
- [ ] markers and fabric trims
- [ ] tape and glue

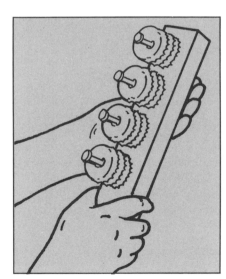

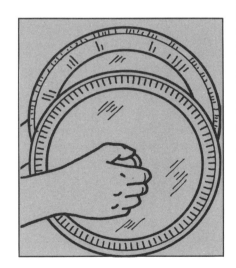

# Befriend the Elderly

**THINGS YOU'LL NEED:**
- [ ] invitation

**OPTIONAL:**
- [ ] refreshments
- [ ] transportation
- [ ] bulletins, church magazines, Sunday school material, large-print Bibles

Select one or more of the following activities to do with your group.

## Nursing Home Day

Plan a special nursing home day at your church. Kids might present a special program, such as "Channel 7, 'I Witness' News," for the residents. Send an invitation to the nursing home, and then offer assistance in transporting the residents to the church. Plan to have a social time after the program for refreshment and visiting. This will help to make it an outing your guests will remember.

## Plan Interesting Programs

Children might present a worship service at the nursing home. If so, try using audiovisual materials. The elderly are not accustomed to seeing flannelgraphs or object lessons as part of the presentations. Also keep the message short and interesting.

Most folks enjoy music and children. Special numbers and favorite hymns help lift the spirit.

Keep your presentation flexible, allowing for minor disruptions. Assist patients in need or call for a staff member. After the service, take time to greet residents individually. Personal contact means so much.

## How to Be a Good Visitor

Before visiting a nursing home, give children the following guidelines:

1. Respect the people's property and rooms; you are a guest in their home.
2. Be willing to listen to repeated stories. Don't be afraid to ask questions.
3. Be considerate of the facility's policies and procedures. Feel free to ask the staff questions regarding the home or the care of a resident.
4. If a patient seems confused, gently remind him or her of facts such as name, place, and day.
5. Speak slowly and distinctly. Explain to the visually impaired what you are doing and what is going on around them.
6. Make short, more frequent visits.

## Ask Their Help

Invite nursing residents to help with your church's service projects. Some will enjoy contributing their talents to create posters, banners, and wall hangings, to sew costumes for plays, or to write articles, type, or send greeting cards. Be sure to give them ample time to complete their part of the projects.

## Nix a Holiday Visit?

Holidays can be special times in the nursing home. But they can be overdone. For example, how would you feel if you were in a home and this were the twelfth group running through singing carols as their December service project?

Try substituting visits and programs at other times of the year. The residents can provide wonderful audiences for dress rehearsals of plays, concert, and entertaining programs.

## Stay in Touch

Keep in regular contact with shut-ins. Take them cassettes of recorded services and special programs that occurred at church. Recorded personalized messages from their friends would be very meaningful, especially birthday greetings and a group singing "Happy Birthday" to them on their special day. Other things to include on cassettes could be children singing and reciting, special music by the choir, and get-well greetings from their church family.

Cards and greetings from children would also brighten their day.

## Part of God's Family

Highlight a different senior adult or shut-in every week in the children's worship time. Mention the person's name, show a picture, and give a short biography. Remember the person's special prayer needs. Encourage children to write short greetings and deliver them. Such thoughtfulness reminds them that God's family cares. ∎

*by Dale Cope*

# II.
# READINGS, SKITS, AND PUPPETS

# In the Beginning

## A Scripture-based Choral Reading Celebrating God's Creation

**THINGS YOU'LL NEED:**

- ☐ scripts (about 6 copies)
- ☐ music

**OPTIONAL:**

- ☐ old bed sheet or butcher paper
- ☐ chalk or pastels

### By David and Becca Toht

This choral reading can help students learn and appreciate the creation story in an exciting, effective way. A choral reading allows the story to be experienced by hearing it, visualizing it, singing appropriate music, and participating in readings.

A choral reading is not very different from a choir presentation. Instead of singing the words, the words are spoken together by the whole group, by solos, duets, all boys, etc. (Two children with softer voices might read as a duet instead of a solo.) Words may be said quietly or loudly, slowly or quickly, with happy, smiling voices or sad voices—it all depends upon the meaning of what is being read.

This presentation could be done effectively in the adult worship service or to any audience after it has been adequately rehearsed. You might want to rehearse it every Sunday for several weeks. (This also helps the students learn the Creation story.) Students could draw a large backdrop depicting the Creation events. You could use an old white sheet or a wide roll of butcher paper. Soft chalk or pastels work well on this kind of project. The artwork could be done by interested students during part of each session.

Divide students into Chorus 1 and Chorus 2. Point out that every time the choruses say lines, they are to be in the "hands on each others' shoulders" position.

# In the Beginning

**THE FIRST DAY**

**Sing "This Is My Father's World."**

**All:** In the beginning, God created.

**Narrator 1:** The earth was dark and as bare as a ball of clay. An icy, cold wind blew without stopping.

**Narrator 2:** Not a bird chirped. No leaves rustled. Not a waterfall splashed. All was silent and empty.

(Pause)

**Solo 1:** The God said, "Let there be light." And the earth was bathed in golden light.

**Solo 2:** The light was warm and full of life. Where there was nothing at all, God had made something!

**All:** Praise the great Creator!

**Chorus 1:** God was pleased with what He made.

**Chorus 2:** There was day and night—the first day.

**THE SECOND DAY**

**All:** In the beginning, God created.

**Narrator 1:** God said, "There will be clouds in the sky and oceans on the earth."

**Narrator 2:** And so on the second day, He made blue sky. The clouds moved slowly in the sky like huge mountains.

**Solo 1:** Lord, how beautiful is Your creation!

**Solo 2:** How wonderful is Your world!

**All:** Lord, You have made so many things. How wisely You have made them!

**Chorus 1:** God was pleased with what He made.

**Chorus 2:** There was day and night—the second day.

**THE THIRD DAY**

**Sing "For the Beauty of the Earth."**

**All:** In the beginning, God created.

**Narrator 1:** On the third day God pulled dry land from the bottom of the sea and arranged it as it pleased Him.

**Narrator 2:** He pushed mountains up from the depths of the earth and scooped out valleys.

**Solo 1:** He let the waves of the waters dig out harbors and coves. He called the waters "seas."

**Solo 2:** No place looked exactly the same as another.

**Chorus 1:** He rules over the deserts and jungles.

**Chorus 2:** He rules over the mountains and seashores.

**All:** Praise the great Creator!

INTERPRETIVE MOVEMENT

Students stand in a row or semicircle, arms outstretched facing audience, hands and heads down.

Raise arms, fingers spread, faces up, smiling.

Lower hands to each other's shoulders. (This chorus movement will be repeated periodically.)

Chorus 1 raise arms and sway back and forth. Chorus 2 make wave motions with hands.

(Repeat hands-on-shoulders movement)

Chorus 1 mimic molding mountains. Chorus 2 mimic scooping out valleys.

(Repeat hands-on-shoulders movement)

**Narrator 1:** God commanded all sorts of plants and trees to grow on the land, and they sprang up to His glory.
**Narrator 2:** Bright colors splashed across the fields and mountains. Sweet fragrances drifted in the breeze.
**Solo 1:** God made bluebells, now white daisies, and sunny meadows of sweet clover.
**Solo 2:** Waving pines and swinging vines—there was green the world over.
**Chorus 1:** God was pleased with what He made.
**Chorus 2:** There was day and night—the third day.

## THE FOURTH DAY

**All:** In the beginning, God created.
**Narrator 1:** God created lights to mark day and night, and to signal the seasons.
**Narrator 2:** The greater light, the sun, ruled the day. The smaller light, the moon, ruled the night.
**Narrator 1:** Then God scattered the stars across the sky.
**Narrator 2:** He set the planets in their courses.
**Solo 1:** Praise Him, sun and moon!
**Solo 2:** Praise Him, shining stars!
**All:** Praise Him, highest heavens!
**Chorus 1:** God was pleased with what He made.
**Chorus 2:** There was day and night—the fourth day.

## THE FIFTH DAY

**All:** In the beginning, God created.
**Narrator 1:** Churning the waters of the oceans, God created sea creatures, saying,
**Solo 1:** "Let the seas teem with fish—porpoise and whales, sea urchins and snails—all things that live under the water."
**Solo 2:** "Let the air come alive with birds."
**Narrator 2:** To the creatures of the sea and sky God said,
**Solo 1:** "Have babies! Increase your numbers!"
**Solo 2:** "Fill the ocean and sky with baby creatures just like you!"
**Chorus 1:** Lord, how beautiful is Your creation!
**Chorus 2:** How wonderful is Your world!
**All:** Lord, You have made so many things. How wisely You have made them!
**Chorus 1:** God was pleased with what He made.
**Chorus 2:** There was day and night—the fifth day.

### INTERPRETIVE MOVEMENT

All squat down. Chorus 1 shoots up quickly, arms up, and sway. Chorus 2 "grows" slowly, wiggling fingers around heads.

(Repeat hands-on-shoulders movement)

Raise arms over head in a circle.

Raise hands and wave them, wiggling fingers in twinkling fashion.

(Repeat hands-on-shoulders movement)

Chorus 1 clasp hands together to make a fish shape and pretend the fish are jumping over waves. Chorus 2 flap hands like birds.

(Repeat hands-on-shoulders movement)

16

## THE SIXTH DAY

**Sing "All Things Bright and Beautiful."**
**All:** In the beginning, God created.
**Narrator 1:** Turning to the land, God said, "From the earth let wild animals and livestock be created."
**Narrator 2:** "May each lead his life in his own way and in his own place."
**Solo 1:** God made tortoises, tigers, turtles, and tree frogs; giraffes, gnus, geese and groundhogs.
**Solo 2:** Butterflies and buffalo, badgers, and beagles; antelope, elephants, egrets and eagles.
**Chorus 1:** He rules over the creatures that creep and slither.
**Chorus 2:** He rules over the creatures that leap and run.
**All:** Praise the great Creator!
**Narrator 1:** God said, "Let us make people in our image, to be responsible for the fish, the fowl, and the animals." So God made man and woman.
**Solo 1:** Praise the Lord, for we are His people!
**Solo 2:** Praise the Lord, for He has made us like Himself!
**All:** Praise the great Creator!
**Narrator 2:** God told the people every plant would be theirs for food.
**Solo 1:** God gave them tomatoes and potatoes, turnips, tangerines; broccoli, beets, bananas, and beans.
**Solo 2:** Sweet corn, squash, spinach, and cherries; peanuts, parsnips, and all kinds of berries.
**Chorus 1:** God was pleased with what He made.
**Chorus 2:** There was day and night—the sixth day.

## THE SEVENTH DAY

**All:** In the beginning, God created.
**Narrator 1:** And in the peace of the last day of Creation, God rested. His great work was finished.
**Narrator 2:** He looked with pleasure on all He had made.
**All:** And all was very, very good.
**Solo 1:** God blessed the seventh day, making it holy.
**Solo 2:** Because on it He rested from His work of Creation.
**Chorus 1:** Let us sing for joy to God!
**Chorus 2:** Let us kneel before our Maker!
**All:** Praise the Creator!
**Sing "Let the Whole Creation Cry."** ■

INTERPRETIVE MOVEMENT

Students silently act out different animals—cows lumbering, birds flapping their wings, elephants with trunks swaying, rabbits hopping, turtles creeping around, etc.

(Repeat hands-on-shoulders movement)
Bow heads, arms at sides. Slowly "come alive," lifting heads and raising arms to the sky.

Stretch arms up, pretending to pick fruit from bushes and trees and eat it.

(Repeat hands-on-shoulders movement)

Slowly kneel, rest head on hands.
Remain kneeling. Place arms on each other's shoulders, smiling.
Chorus 1 leaps up, hands in the air. Then Chorus 2 does the same.
Everyone come together in front and hold hands to sing final song.

# PUPPET PATTERNS

**THINGS
YOU'LL
NEED:**
- [ ] **copies of puppet patterns**
- [ ] **scissors**
- [ ] **glue**
- [ ] **paper bags**
- [ ] **yarn**
- [ ] **fabric**

Your students can make these easy puppets with a few fabric scraps and paper bags.

Make copies of the puppet heads. Cut them out and glue them to the bottoms of two paper bags. The bottom of the paper bag, when left slightly folded, functions as the mouth of the puppet (see diagram below). Then glue on yarn for hair and fabric for clothing.

Display your puppet and show children how it can talk by placing your fingers behind the head and moving it up and down. Say a few words in a puppet voice such as, "Hi, kids, my name is Adam."

Have each child cut out a puppet head and glue it to the bottom of a paper bag. Provide children with materials to individualize their puppets. When children move the heads of their puppets up and down, the puppets will seem to be talking. ■

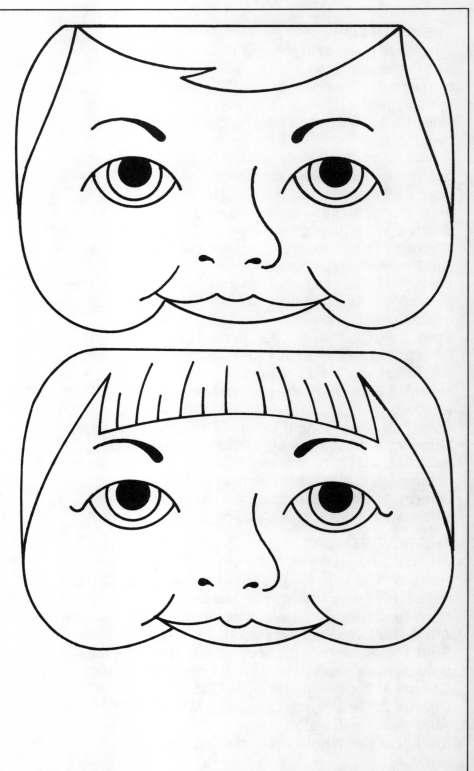

# PUPPET STAGE

## by Annie and Steve Wamberg

Need a puppet stage? Try one of these simple ideas.

☐ If your time and resources are limited, make a stage by draping a sheet over a table. Kids can kneel down behind the table and hold their puppets over the edge.

☐ You (or one of the families) can also make a simple cardboard stage. You'll need two refrigerator boxes for this stage. You will be making the right side of the stage from one box and the left side from the other box. Cut the inside side from each box, and most of the back. Leave about six inches at the top on the back for stability. Don't leave any cardboard on the side or bottom of the back because it would get in the way of your puppeteers. Be sure to leave the bottoms in the boxes or your stage will lose its shape.

The basic measurements are given in the drawings. The stage opening should be about four and one-half feet high. You might want to adjust the height if your students are exceptionally short or tall.

Make your opening as wide as you can. Three inches on each side will give enough support.

Duct tape works well to fasten the boxes together. You may also want to reinforce the stage with furring strips along the edges of the opening, at the bottom along the front, and at the top across the back.

Lighting for puppetry is important. You'll want to check out the lighting available in the room in which you will be performing. Lighting from the front is best, but lighting from overhead will work if the top is removed from the stage.

Stage Scenery: If you're planning to perform these sketches for an audience, you'll want to make some scenery for your puppet stage. Have some of your teens who are interested start on it now. They'll need to work on it outside of practice time, so be sure they're willing to commit the time.

Look over all the scripts, and decide what scenery you want made. You may be able to use the same scenery for several different scenes.

One good type of scenery is painted paper or cloth rolled on a wooden dowel. A spring-loaded window shade also works well. Either one can be temporarily attached at the top of the stage and the scenery rolled down.

A more 3-D effect can be achieved by painting cardboard or Masonite and attaching it to the stage. It can also be made to stand by itself on a base. ■

**THINGS YOU'LL NEED:**
☐ **bed sheet**
☐ **table**
☐ **2 refrigerator boxes**
☐ **knife**
☐ **ruler**
☐ **paint**
☐ **paintbrushes**
☐ **cardboard or Masonite**
☐ **wooden dowel**

**BACK VIEW**

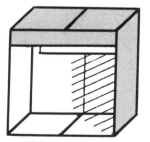

**FRONT VIEW**

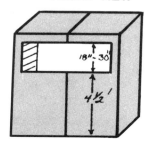

18" – 30"
4½'

# *JOSEPH,*
### THIS IS YOUR LIFE

**THINGS YOU'LL NEED:**
- ☐ tape recorder
- ☐ tape
- ☐ *The Picture Bible*

**OPTIONAL:**
- ☐ musical instruments
- ☐ recording of music, etc.

If a family or group of children likes to act, they might enjoy making a tape recording of the life of Joseph, found on pages 78-106 of *The Picture Bible.* Have them read the story and decide which parts they would like to take.

Appoint a director, who will help each actor with expression. It is also important for each character in the Joseph story to have a distinctive voice. Actors might mark the script with different-colored markers to indicate when each voice should be used.

Sound effects are also important. Can someone mimic the sound of sheep baaing or camels grunting? The jangling of bells may show the approach of the caravan. Music might be used to show that Joseph has gone from a prison to the palace of the Pharaoh. Music might also be used to introduce and conclude the tape. Last, decide who might be master of ceremonies. This person will announce the title of the tape, titles of each chapter in the Joseph story, and cast of characters.

Advertise in the church bulletin or newsletter for help in making the tape recording. Even if your actors have polished their parts, the quality of their production will be diminished by a poor tape recorder. Someone in your church may have excellent equipment and be highly skilled in making a recording. Even if no such person is available, your actors will enjoy putting their acting skills to use.■

—LT

# JOSEPH TV SPECIAL

If the ancient Egyptians had had televisions, they would probably have had a special program on Joseph's life soon after his death. Challenge kids to put on a "Joseph Special" much as they might if they were Egyptian television producers.

Using the following suggestions, have kids divide up parts and prepare scripts.

### GROUP 1: Commentator

Introduce the special by telling the TV audience:

a) The reason for the special. Joseph died today. (For circumstances of his death, read "South into Egypt," pages 101-104, *The Picture Bible*.)

b) Tell about Joseph's major contribution to Egypt. (Read pages 97-106.)

c) Briefly tell how Joseph came to Egypt and rose to power. (Review pages 78-87.)

### GROUP 2: Interview Benjamin

Dress Benjamin in a Bible-time costume of sandals, bathrobe, sash, etc. Review pages 78-106 of *The Picture Bible* to find answers to the following interview questions. You might interview Benjamin with a microphone while he is pretending to hoe his garden.

1) We have heard that Joseph had many brothers who were jealous of him. Would you tell us about that?

2) What was your relationship with Joseph?

3) We have heard that you played a key role in Joseph's revealing his identity to his other brothers. Explain what happened.

4) Why did you admire your older brother Joseph so much?

### GROUP 3: Interview a Dream Expert

Introduce Dr. Dramadream. You might begin the interview by saying that Joseph's uncanny ability to interpret dreams had a significant part to play in his gaining power in Egypt. Dr. Dramadream has written a book on Joseph's dreams called *Joseph, the Dreamer*. Research Joseph's dreams in Genesis 37:5-11; 40:9-23; 41:16-34. Review also *The Picture Bible*, pages 80, 86, 87.

For visual effect, make up cards that summarize each dream (you might draw a picture to represent

## THINGS YOU'LL NEED:

- [ ] **Hebrew costumes (bathrobes, sandals, sashes)**
- [ ] **hoe or rake**
- [ ] **Egyptian woman's costume (robe, headband)**
- [ ] **paper cards**
- [ ] **microphones**
- [ ] **chairs**
- [ ] **man dressed to look like a professor**
- [ ] **felt-tipped markers**
- [ ] **Bible dictionary or encyclopedia**

## OPTIONAL:

- [ ] **videotape equipment**

plants, heavenly bodies, etc., instead of using words) as well as the person who had the dream:
DREAM ABOUT PLANTS—JOSEPH;
DREAM ABOUT SUN, MOON, AND STARS—JOSEPH;
DREAM ABOUT GRAPES—BUTLER;
DREAM ABOUT BIRDS—BAKER;
DREAM ABOUT COWS—KING

Using the visual aids, ask Dr. Dramadream to explain

**a) Who dreamed what;**

**b) How Joseph interpreted each dream;**

**c) Results of Joseph's interpretation;**

**d) Where Joseph said he got his unusual power.**

**GROUP 4: Joseph's Religion**
For answers to the following questions, look in a Bible encyclopedia, Bible dictionary, and *The Picture Bible*. Dress Joseph's wife to look something like her picture on page 88 in *The Picture Bible*, if possible. Discuss her husband's religion. Introduce Joseph's wife by saying that she is the daughter of the priest of On. Ask the following questions:

**1. It has been said that your husband had an unusual religion. How is it different from our Egyptian practice of worshiping many gods?**
**2. Explain why Joseph's religion has been called a family religion. (She might show a picture of Joseph's family tree, activity piece 2A in the Leader's Guide, and discuss God's promise to Abraham.)**
**3. Joseph is said to have received his ability to interpret dreams from his God. Would you explain that, please?**
**4. Joseph was said to be an** outstanding leader. **How did Joseph's religious beliefs affect his personality?**
**5. Before his death, your husband called in his children to receive the family blessing. What is this blessing for?**

Close the interview by recommending everyone to read Dr. Dramadream's new book.

**Conclusion**
Conclude the "Joseph TV Special" as if your were standing out in the Land of Goshen, the richest farmland in Egypt. Explain that Joseph's family has increased both in size and wealth. It remains to be seen whether the Hebrews, as they are called, will stay in Egypt or return to the Land of Promise that their God promised to give them. ■

—LT

# Crown and Mustache Props

☐ **yellow or gold construction paper**
☐ **scraps of brightly colored paper**
☐ **scissors**
☐ **glue**

**OPTIONAL:**
☐ **glitter**
☐ **metallic rickrack**

Have children draw around the crown pattern on gold or yellow construction paper. Then ask them to cut it out and glue on "jewels" from colored pieces of construction paper. They may add a little more sparkle by gluing glitter or glittery rickrack around the edges. Cut two 2″ x 9″ strips of construction paper for each child. Staple one strip to one side of the crown, and staple the other to the other side of the crown. Place the crown on the child's head, and adjust to size. Then staple the strips together. ■

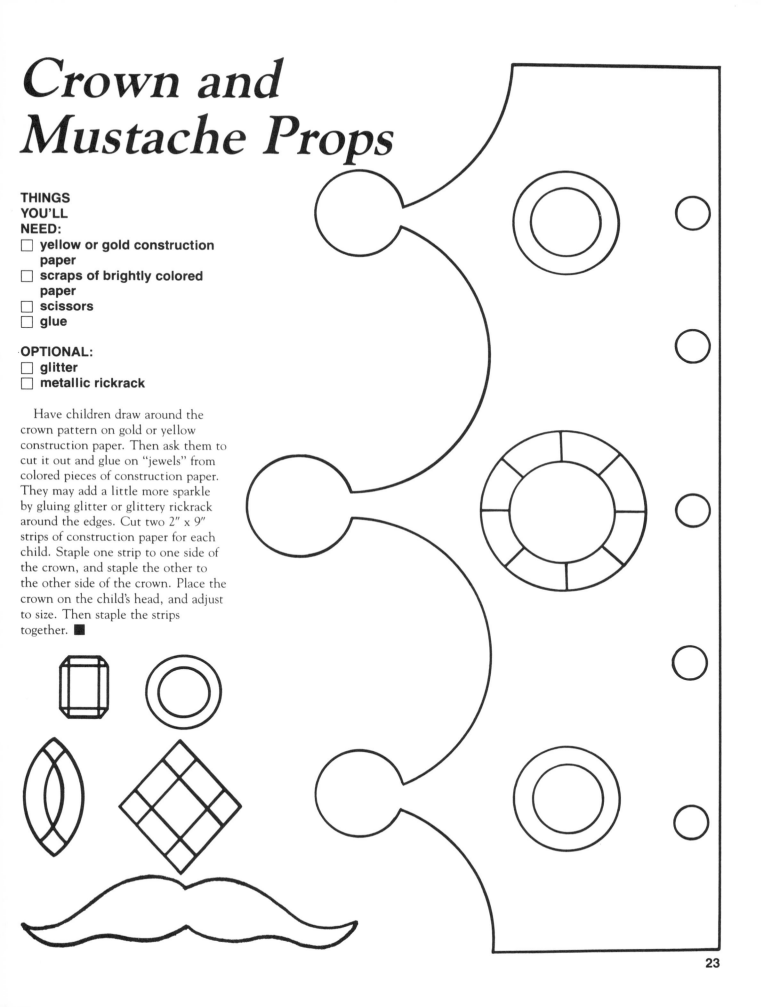

# CHANNEL 7
# *'I Witness' News*

**Newscaster #1:** Good evening. This is _____ with Channel 7 "I Witness" News. Tonight in the headlines young Saul had to face his first big decision as king of Israel. Three days ago the people from Ammon (point to white area of "Divided Kingdom" map) threatened the city of Jabesh. They were planning to punch out an eye of every man in the city. King Saul needed to get his army to fight back, but they did not want to fight. The king had to threaten to kill their oxen before they would decide to join his army. However, the army managed to surprise the people of Ammon by attacking at dawn. Saul's army won the battle.

And now, we'll hear a report from _____.

**Newscaster #2:** Thank you, _____.

In other news tonight, Samuel, the old judge of Israel, gave a good-bye speech in the town square. Samuel's closing words were, "Obey the Lord and serve your king, and all will be well with you. But if you return to any of your wicked ways, you shall be destroyed—both you and your king!"

And now, we'll hear a report from _____.

**Newscaster #3:** Thank you, _____.

We have just received word that Saul's army attacked the Philistines. The soldiers had been waiting for Samuel to offer a sacrifice to God before they started to fight, but Samuel was late getting there. So Saul offered the sacrifice himself! When Samuel did come he was furious at Saul for disobeying God. We regret that we were not able to cover the meeting live. However, we will now take you to our field reporter in Gilgal where Saul's army has just attacked the Amalekites.

**Field Reporter** (*standing away from table, will need some kind of microphone. As he is introduced, there could be a faint sound of sheep bleating*)**:** Thank you, _____.

I'm here at Gilgal where Saul's army has just defeated the Amalekites. It's quiet here in the camp. The soldiers are resting after the battle, but we have just heard a strange noise coming from Saul's tent. (*Samuel enters, heads in direction of the noise.*) Wait a minute. Here comes Samuel. We will ask him what is going on. (*Calls out.*) Samuel, Samuel. (*Samuel pauses.*) Excuse me. I'm _____ with the Channel 7 "I Witness" News team, and you're on the air. Would you mind telling us what that noise is?

## THINGS YOU'LL NEED:
☐ table
☐ "Divided Kingdom" map
☐ five copies of script

*The front of the room should be set up like a newsroom. Student newscasters may sit behind a table and read their parts. Fill in the first names of the student readers in the appropriate blanks.*

**Samuel:** Right now I'm not sure what that noise is, but I'm on my way to find out.

*(Sheep bleat again.)*

**Reporter:** Wait a minute, sir. It sounded like sheep. *(Sheep bleat again.)* Yes—there it is again. Unmistakable. Why does Saul have sheep inside his tent?

**Samuel:** He must have stolen them from the Amalekites when he defeated them. If so, he's in hot water!

**Reporter:** What do you mean? Doesn't God usually let the armies keep things from the lands they conquer?

**Samuel:** Yes, but this time God gave specific instructions that we shouldn't keep anything.

**Reporter:** Mr. Samuel, have you thought about what you will say to Saul when you see him?

**Samuel:** I'm afraid that I will have to tell him that he will be replaced as king. *(Samuel walks away sadly toward Saul's tent.)*

**Reporter:** There you have it, folks. Samuel has just said that Saul will not be king much longer. It appears that Saul is in big trouble for disobeying God. We will keep you posted on any further developments. This has been _____ in Gilgal. And now—back to _____ (Reporter number one).

**Newcaster #1:** Thank you, _____ .

That concludes our news for tonight. I'm _____. From all of us at Channel 7 "I Witness" News, goodnight! ∎

—EP

# Friendship Pantomime

ALONE—sits by himself or herself, looks lonely and bored, as if waiting for someone.

One by one the following actors (either boys or girls) pass by. They portray various sorts of "friends."

AVOIDER—walks from stage right and when sees "Alone," he or she goes by, pretending not to see.

MOCKER—walks from left to right, stops near "Alone" and laughs. Says, "Man, what is wrong with you? Don't you have any friends?" Laughs again and walks off.

TOO BUSY—walks quickly from right to left, stopping abruptly at "Need." He or she looks down and says, "I'll come back and be your friend later, if there is time." Looks at watch and then walks off hurriedly.

TRUE FRIEND—walks directly toward "Alone." Sits down next to him or her and asks, "What's your name?"

"Alone" smiles and they pretend to have a conversation as the skit ends.

# THE SHEPHERD KING

## Musical Program on the Life of David

**THINGS YOU'LL NEED:**

- [ ] **Bible-time costumes (bathrobes or short tunics, shawls, and sandals). Boy David may wear a short tunic and sandals. In Acts Two and Three, David and Jonathan will be dressed primarily in armor. Saul and the soldiers should also wear armor and carry swords, which can be made from aluminum foil and cardboard.**
- [ ] **props include a harp made from cardboard and string, a cloth or burlap sack filled with rags or newspaper, David's sling for Act One; David's harp, Saul's spear, Saul's throne, David's bow and arrow, and an imitation rock for Act Two; small jug or cup and piece of bread for Act Three.**
- [ ] **about 10 copies of the script**

**OPTIONAL:**

- [ ] **puppets, patterns on page 18 of this book**
- [ ] **puppet stage, directions on page 19 of this book**

### By Jeron Ashford Frame

This musical play dramatizes the life of David from his battle with Goliath up to his coronation as king of Israel.

If your group is small, consider using the script for a puppet show. Tack the script to puppet stage, and assign several parts to each puppeteer. Simple puppets and a puppet stage can be made.

### Cast:

- [ ] The boy, David
- [ ] The man, David
- [ ] The old man, David
- [ ] David's brothers (3)
- [ ] Goliath
- [ ] Saul
- [ ] Jonathan
- [ ] servant
- [ ] girl
- [ ] several townspeople
- [ ] at least 3 soldiers
- [ ] sick man
- [ ] messenger
- [ ] priest
- [ ] The role of Goliath could be assigned to a tall teen or adult who would tower over the rest of the cast.

Students who do not have any of the roles specified above may participate in the musical choir.

### Setting

Adapt the movement of actors to your facilities. The choir should sit in an area close to the platform where the scenes will be enacted—perhaps in the choir loft. Students playing parts will leave the choir when they are in a scene and return to the choir when their scene is over.

No special scenery is needed since the location of each scene is different. The setup of your stage area will determine the best way for actors to enter and exit.

### Music

The program includes five songs, all based on psalms of David. These songs are found in *Worship Time Music Book*, published by David C. Cook. Use piano accompaniment (and other instruments if you choose).

Act One begins with David singing "You Know, Lord," page 19. This is suggested as a solo, but you may wish to have the choir sing along. The act ends with everyone singing "Sing for Joy," page 18, as they celebrate David's victory over Goliath. "You Know, Lord" repeats in Act Two. The song is interrupted when Saul throws a spear at David. Only David should sing this short section. Act Two ends with "I Need You and You Need Me," page 15. Jonathan begins this song and is joined by David and the choir.

Everyone sings "My Deliverer," page 9, after the women and children are rescued from the wicked Amalakites. Children play tambourines and other rhythm instruments as they parade down the aisles during this song. Later, in Act Two, David sings "Lord, I Am Crying," page 32. The choir may join him if necessary.

The program ends with "Sing for Joy," page 18, during which children come to the platform for the finale.

# THE SHEPHERD KING

## Musical Program on the Life of David

**ACT ONE**

*(Old David enters slowly, carrying a harp. He looks around at the audience.)*

**Old David:** Hello. I'm glad you're here. *(Holds up harp.)* I haven't played this harp for years. *(Strums a little; chuckles.)* I used to play and sing for King Saul. That was before God made me king of Israel. *(Shakes head.)* When I was a boy tending sheep, I never dreamed of becoming king. But you never know what might happen when you let the Lord lead you! *(Exit.)*

*(Music for "You Know, Lord," begins. David enters with a sack over his shoulder and sings the song. He walks around, shades his eyes, and looks in the distance as if looking for his brothers. He might do actions to go with the song such as pointing to himself on the word "we"; to his head on the word "thoughts," etc. After the song, his three brothers and soldiers enter, stand at edge of stage, and look worried.)*

**David:** Hi, guys! Father sent me with food for you. *(Sets sack down.)*

**Brother 1:** Thanks, Little Brother.

*(Goliath's voice heard roaring offstage.)*

**Goliath:** Come out and fight me!

*(Soldiers back off muttering fearfully.)*

**David:** Wow! Who's that?

**Brother 1:** That's Goliath, the Philistine. He's challenging our men to fight.

**Brother 2:** But everyone is afraid of him. He's so big! In fact, Goliath is a giant!

**Goliath** *(calls loudly from offstage)*: Come on, cowards! Who will fight me?

*(Soldiers all cringe. Some run offstage; others fall to the ground in fear.)*

**Soldier** *(to David)*: Saul is offering a big reward for the man who kills Goliath.

**David:** I'm not afraid of any giant! God is on our side! What is the reward?

**Brother 3** *(angrily)*: David! Mind your own business! You shouldn't be here!

**David** *(offended)*: Well, can't I even ask a simple question?

**Soldier:** Whoever kills Goliath will be rewarded and get to marry Saul's daughter.

*(Saul enters with a few soldiers. Goliath roars again. David's brothers, along with several of the soldiers, run offstage in fear. David walks over to Saul.)*

**David:** King Saul, we should not be afraid of Goliath. I will fight him, sir!

**Saul:** You're just a boy.

**David:** I'm a shepherd, sir. Lions and bears have tried to eat my sheep. But I fought and killed them. God helped me do it. He will help me kill Goliath, too.

**Saul:** Go ahead then. And may God protect you from the giant.

*(David walks slowly toward center stage, carrying his sling and picking up rocks. Saul and soldiers exit. Goliath enters from the other side. He sees David; laughs.)*

**Goliath:** What do you want, little boy? Are you going to chase me with a stick, as though I were a dog? *(Laughs again.)*

**David:** You have a sword, but I have God. Today I will defeat you. Then everyone will know that Israel has a mighty God.

*(Goliath roars with laughter, while David loads his sling and winds up. Goliath suddenly notices what David is doing.)*

**Goliath** *(roars)*: I'll tear you to pieces!

*(Goliath tries to grab David as the rock hits his forehead. He jerks back from the impact and yells; then crashes to the ground. David's brothers and soldiers enter.)*

**Brother 2:** David did it! Our little brother killed Goliath!

*(All cheer and sing "Sing for Joy." The soldiers raise David on their shoulders and carry him around the stage while they sing. After the song, they put David down. Saul enters and shakes David's hand.)*

**Saul:** Well done, boy.

**David:** Thank you, sir.

**Soldier 1:** All right, men. Let's go get those Philistines!

**All:** Hurray! The Lord lives. Down with the Philistines!

*(All exit running and cheering.)*

### ACT TWO

*(Old David enters.)*

**Old David:** King Saul was pretty impressed with me after I killed Goliath. He even took me to live with him in the palace. The best thing about that was getting to know Saul's son, Jonathan. *(Sits down on edge of stage and smiles.)* Jonathan was my very best friend. We did everything together—we ate, played, and even fought battles together. *(Frowns and gets up; walks slowly around the stage while talking.)* But something happened to Saul. He stopped obeying God. *(Sighs heavily and exits.)*

*(David and soldiers process in; gather in front of stage. Townspeople cheer David and gather around him. Saul enters, standing off to the side, watching the celebration.)*

**Girl:** Saul has beaten thousands of enemies in battle, but David—*ten* thousand!

*(All exit cheering, except Saul, who paces angrily talking to himself.)*

**Saul:** It's not fair! They say David is a better soldier than I. He could take over my kingdom! I've got to get rid of him.

*(David enters.)*

**David:** King Saul, the Philistines are defeated! We've driven them off!

**Saul:** Very good, young David. *(Walks to throne and sits down.)* Come, play some music for me to celebrate the victory.

*(David picks up his harp from the edge of the stage and sits down on the floor by Saul. David sings "You Know, Lord." While singing, he gets up and walks around the stage. While his back is turned, Saul picks up a spear. He throws it at David just as David turns around. David ducks, stares at Saul in amazement, and runs offstage right.)*

**Saul:** I'll get him yet!

*(Saul exits angrily from the other side of the stage. Jonathan enters; sits on stage cleaning his armor. David runs in.)*

**David:** Jonathan!

**Jonathan:** What's wrong?

**David:** Jonathan, your father the king is trying to kill me.

**Jonathan:** My father would never do anything like that without telling me first.

**David:** He hasn't told you because we're friends!

**Jonathan:** I'll find out for sure if my father wants to kill you. You go hide behind that big rock near the palace. After I see him, I'll come and tell you what to do.

**David:** Be careful. Your father might find out you've warned me.

**Jonathan** *(thinks quietly for a moment)*: Hmm. *(Brightens.)* I have a plan! If everything is all right, I will shoot some arrows close by. But if it isn't, I will shoot them farther away.

*(They exit. David enters and hides behind*

the rock. Jonathan and a servant enter from the other side with a bow and arrow.)

**Jonathan:** Run and get the arrows after I shoot them.

**Servant:** Yes, sir.

*(Jonathan shoots an arrow past David. The servant goes and bends to pick it up.)*

**Jonathan:** Didn't the arrow go farther than that?

**David** *(whispers softly to himself):* That's my signal!

*(The servant brings back the arrow.)*

**Jonathan:** Please take these back to the city. *(Hands him bow and arrow. Servant exits. David runs out from his hiding place.)*

**Jonathan:** Oh, David, it's really true! My father is planning to have you killed.

**David:** What am I going to do?

**Jonathan:** You've got to leave. I'll help you.

**David:** I'm glad you're my friend.

*(Jonathan, David, and the choir sing "I Need You and You Need Me." Jonathan and David shake hands.)*

**David:** Promise we'll be best friends forever.

**Jonathan:** I promise.

*(They exit in different directions.)*

## ACT THREE
*(Old David enters.)*

**Old David:** After that, I was a fugitive. Everywhere I went, Saul sent soldiers to try to kill me. After a while, I had my own army and my own city to look after. But even though Saul hated me, I still loved him. He was my king and the father of my best friend. *(Pauses.)* Being the leader of so many people was hard. I remember one very bad day. We were on our way back from a battle, and we saw a glow in the distance. Our

town, Ziklag, was on fire! *(Exits.)*

*(David and several soldiers walk slowly on stage, looking in horror all around them.)*

**Soldier 1:** I can't believe it! The whole city is destroyed!

**Soldier 2:** Who could've done this?

*(Another soldier runs in.)*

**Soldier 3:** Our wives and children are gone—captured! It's your fault, David.

*(Soldiers agree, mumbling bitterly. David moves away from the soldiers to front of stage. He sings "Lord, I'm Crying" as a prayer to God. Then returns to his men.)*

**David** *(to his soldiers):* We've got to find these robbers! God will help us!

*(All rush offstage in different directions. The sick man enters and lies down near center stage. A few moments later the soldiers reenter as a group, walking across the stage as though down a road.)*

**Soldier 1:** David, look! *(Points to man.)* He might know about the robbers!

*(All gather around the man and try to help him up.)*

**Soldier 2:** He's sick. I think he's starving.

**David:** Give him some food and water. As soon as he's able to talk, we'll ask him some questions.

*(Soldiers give the man a bite or two of bread and a sip of water. He slowly sits up.)*

**David:** Who are you? What happened?

**Sick Man** *(weakly):* I'm a slave. I was there with the Amalakites when they destroyed Ziklag.

**Soldier 1** *(turns to another soldier):* The Amalakites! So that's who did it!

**Sick Man:** My master left me here to die.

**David:** Do you know where they are now?

**Sick Man:** I'll take you to their camp if you promise to protect me.

*(Soldiers help the sick man up.)*

**Soldier 2:** We'll get those Amalakites!

**Soldier 1:** And get our wives and children back, too!

*(All exit. Moments later David enters from side of stage with a few soldiers talking among themselves. Suddenly several soldiers, women, and children run in from other side of stage.)*

**Soldier 1:** David! David! The Amalakites are defeated!

**Soldier 2:** And our families are safe!

**David:** Praise the Lord! He answered my prayer for help.

*(Several soldiers and women and children hug, cheer, and cry happily. All sing "My Deliverer." Toward the end of the song, actors may run offstage and down aisles while singing. All return to the choir, leaving David alone on stage. David sits on edge of stage, looking worried. A servant enters.)*

**Servant:** David, is something wrong?

**David:** I'm just a little worried about Saul and Jonathan. I haven't heard anything about them for such a long time. I hope . . .

**Servant:** There's a messenger waiting outside. I think he might know something about King Saul and Jonathan.

*(Servant exits and messenger enters.)*

**Messenger:** Good day, David. I come from the battle. I have some news for you.

**David** *(jumping up):* What is it?

**Messenger:** King Saul is dead.

**David** *(stunned):* What about Jonathan?

**Messenger:** He's dead, too.

**David** *(facing audience, in shock):* My king and my best friend, both dead. *(Turns back to messenger.)* You may go.

*(Messenger exits. David sadly sits down.)*

**David** *(loudly):* Oh, Jonathan, you were such a good friend! *(Buries face in hands for a few moments, then looks up suddenly.)* Oh, God, what should I do now? *(Gets up quickly and begins to pace.)* It's safe now for me to go back to Israel. I suppose I should, but . . . *(Looks up toward heaven.)* Oh, Lord God, I feel so sad! *(Sings, "Lord, I Am Crying." Exits slowly.)*

*(Old David enters.)*

**Old David:** I wanted to obey God, but I was afraid. I made lots of mistakes in my life and did wrong things. But I kept trying. God showed me that He had some special plans for me. He also taught me something very important—to be a good leader, you must first be a good follower. *(Exits.)*

*(David and all cast enter happily.)*

**Priest:** Welcome back to Israel, David! We want you to be our new king. We know that God is with you.

*(People shout "Hail, King David" and cheer. Priest lays hands on David's shoulders.)*

**All:** God bless King David! Long live the king!

*(All cheer and gather around David, singing "Sing for Joy." Choir joins in and comes down to the platform while singing. The whole cast may form a procession, led by David, down the aisles.)* ■

# INTERVIEW
## YOUR CHURCH LEADERS

**THINGS
YOU'LL
NEED:**
- [ ] tape recorder
- [ ] photocopies of questions below
- [ ] church leaders

Invite the pastor, choir director, missions chairperson, and other church leaders to become part of a panel. If that is not possible, meet with them individually and tape-record or videotape the interview. You will find directions for making a videotape on page 39 of this book.

Following are suggested questions. You might ask a group of students to select some from among these questions and to conduct the interview.

If the tape is used over several sessions, begin each session by introducing the interviewer and members of the panel.

### Part 1: Meeting God's Leaders
- [ ] What are your main responsibilities as _____ in this church?
- [ ] When you have a decision to make, what steps do you usually take?
- [ ] What are the hardest decisions you've had to make?
- [ ] When do you find it helpful to ask someone's advice before making a decision?
- [ ] When you ask someone for advice, what kind of person do you consider?
- [ ] When people come to you for advice, how do you know what to say?

### Part 2: Being Like Your Leaders
- [ ] When you were a child, did you look up to any special Christian in your church? If so, what did you admire most about this person?
- [ ] Did you try to imitate this person in any way? If so, how?
- [ ] What are some things you have learned by being like other Christians?
- [ ] There are probably people in this church who try to be like you. What is something you hope they will imitate?

## Part 3: Leading in Worship

☐ (to the pastor) Sometimes pastors say that they have received a call from God to become a minister. What do they mean? Did you receive such a call? If so, tell about it.

☐ (to other lay leaders) How did you become involved in church leadership? Did you sense that God was leading you into a specific kind of church leadership? If so, how did you recognize God's leading?

☐ If someone came up and asked why you have a worship service every Sunday, what would you say?

☐ What do you want people to gain from worshiping God together?

☐ How do you plan a worship service?

☐ What part of the worship service do you like to lead best?

☐ What have you learned about making worship meaningful?

☐ How can people in the congregation best contribute to worship?

☐ What advice can you give to kids who want to lead in worship?

## Part 4: Helping Needy People

☐ How do you know when people in this church need help?

☐ What steps do you usually take to help these people?

☐ What are some things our church is doing right now to help people in our community who are treated unfairly?

☐ There are many needy people in the world. How do you decide which of these people to help?

☐ How does our church try to help these needy people around the world?

☐ What can the children do to help meet these needs? ■

—LT

**THINGS YOU'LL NEED:**

- ☐ crown and scepter for king (See page 23 of this book for crown pattern)
- ☐ crown or veil for queen
- ☐ plain robe for Mordecai
- ☐ black ski hats for bad guys
- ☐ five crowd cue cards that read TA-DA!, OOOO/AHHH, BOO, CLAP/CHEER, WEEP/WAIL
- ☐ six copies of script

**CAST:**

- ☐ **King Ahasuerus**
- ☐ **Queen Esther**
- ☐ **Mordecai**
- ☐ **Haman**
- ☐ **two bad guys**
- ☐ **cue card person**

## ACT 1: A PLOT AGAINST THE KING

*(Enter King.)*

**King:** I am King Ahasuerus, King of all Persia. I am rich, I am powerful, and I want to marry the most beautiful woman in the world.

*(Crowd cue card: TA-DA!)*
*(Enter Queen.)*

**Queen:** I am Queen Esther. The King chose me to be Queen of all Persia. I am very honored.

*(Crowd cue card: OOH/AHH)*
*(King and Queen exit. Enter Mordecai.)*

**Mordecai:** I am Queen Esther's cousin. I am a Jew. And so is she. But I am the only one who knows that. I am worried about Esther.

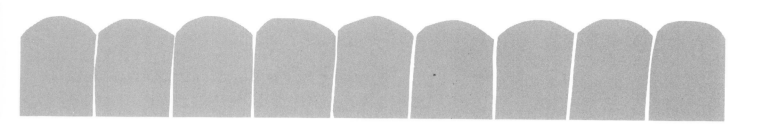

So I come every day to the palace gate, waiting to hear some word about how she is.
(*Sits down in a corner.*)

(*Bad guys enter. They don't see Mordecai.*)
**Bad Guy #1:** I'm tired of being the King's servant.

**Bad Guy #2:** Me, too. Let's get rid of him. I have a plan.
(*Bad guys whisper together. Mordecai listen to their plans. Bad guys exit.*)

**Mordecai** (*calling in loud whisper*): Esther! Esther!
(*Queen enters.*)
**Queen:** What is it, Cousin? Is something wrong?

**Mordecai:** Very wrong! Some servants are planning to kill the King! You must tell him.

(*Mordecai exits. Esther looks worried. King enters.*)
**Queen:** O, King. I have just learned of a plot to kill you.

**King:** Who told you this?

**Queen:** A man named Mordecai, who sits every day by the palace gate. He overheard two of the servants plotting against you. Mordecai told me to warn you.

**King:** I will have those two bad servants punished immediately! But Mordecai has done me a great favor. Have a scribe write this deed in the records of the kingdom. It must not be forgotten.

(*Crowd cue card: CLAP/CHEER*)

## ACT 2: HAMAN PLOTS AGAINST THE JEWS
(*Enter Mordecai and sits in a corner. Enter Haman who struts his stuff.*)
**Haman:** I am the King's new Prime Minister. My name is Haman. I think I'm pretty hot stuff. All the people bow down when I walk in the street.

(*Crowd cue card: BOO!*)

(*Sees Mordecai.*) Wait a minute. There's somebody who isn't bowing to me. Hey, you! Why aren't you bowing down to the King's Prime Minister? Who are you, anyway?

**Mordecai:** I am Mordecai. I am a Jew. We Jews don't bow down to anybody except our God. (*Mordecai exits.*)

**Haman:** Oh! That makes me so mad! I'm going to make Mordecai pay for this!

*(Enter King.)*

**Haman:** O, King. You are so wonderful, great, powerful, and rich, too. But did you know that the Jews in this country don't respect you? As Prime Minister, I would like to make a law to get rid of every Jew. That way they won't be any trouble for you.

*(Crowd cue card: BOO!)*

**King:** What a good idea. You have my permission to kill all the Jews. By the way, Haman, what should I do to honor a man who has pleased me very much?

**Haman** *(to audience)*: O, goody, goody. The King is going to honor me for being such a fantastic person and loyal subject. *(to King)* O, King, let him wear one of your royal robes, and ride your royal horse, and tell one of your nobles to lead him around the city telling everyone that this is the way the King honors those that please him.

**King:** What a good idea! Get a robe and the horse and do exactly as you have suggested—for Mordecai, who sits by the palace gate. He once saved by life, and I want to honor him.

*(Crowd cue card: CLAP/CHEER)*
*(King exits.)*

**Haman:** Oh! That makes me so mad! I'm so mad that I can't wait to kill Mordecai with all the other Jews. I'm going to make a gallows to hang him on.

*(Crowd cue card: BOO!)*

## ACT 3: ESTHER SAVES THE DAY
*(Enter Mordecai, sits in a corner, hands over his face. Enter Queen.)*

**Queen:** Cousin! What's the matter? You should be happy after the way the King honored you, making Haman lead you around the city on the royal horse.

**Mordecai:** I am mourning because Haman is going to kill all the Jews.

*(Crowd cue card: WEEP/WAIL)*

**Esther:** Oh, no. What can we do?

**Mordecai:** You must go the King and ask him to spare the Jews.

**Esther:** But if I go to the King before he calls me, I might die. He doesn't even know that I'm a Jew. . . . Still, it's the only way.

*(Esther and Mordecai exit.)*

*(Enter the King and Haman. Esther enters and kneels down before the King.)*

**King:** Esther! Don't you know it's dangerous to come to the throne room unless I call you? You must have something very important to tell me. Rise, I will not hurt you.

**Esther:** I want to invite you and Haman to a banquet.

**King:** We will come. *(Esther and the King exit.)*

**Haman** *(to audience)*: O, goody, goody. Queen Esther has invited me to a banquet with just her and the King. I must be very important. *(Haman exits.)*

*(Crowd cue card: BOO!)*
*(Enter Esther, King, and Haman.)*

**King:** That was a wonderful banquet, Queen Esther. But you didn't risk coming to the throne room just to ask me to dinner. What do you want?

**Queen:** I want to ask you to spare the lives of my people.

**King:** But who would harm you and your people?

**Queen:** Haman would! He has given an order for all the Jews to be killed, and I am a Jew! He also made a gallows, and he wants to hang my cousin Mordecai on it. You remember Mordecai, the man you honored for saving you life!

**King:** Forget it, Haman! You are a wicked, wicked man. You are going to hang on the gallows you made for Mordecai, and I am going to save the Jews. ∎

—NJ

# SHADOW DRAMA

One creative way to review Bible stories is to do shadow dramas.

### Shadow Directions:

Stretch a sheet tightly from the floor to the ceiling. Place a strong light (100 watts or more) on the floor behind the sheet. Players should stand between the lights and the sheet, and stand frozen during the whole time their picture is on stage. The light should be switched off while the scenes are changed.

### Story Directions:

List Bible stories children have read during the unit, and have kids help you select one they would like to perform.

Divide the story into scenes.

Decide what props you'll need. Some could be cut out of cardboard. Remember that detail is not important since everything will be in shadows.

**Example:** Baby Moses (Exodus 1—2:9)

**Props:** Basket, large bush or tree, doll

**Scenes:**

1. Soldiers pulling baby from mother.
2. Moses' mother hiding him.
3. Moses' mother and sister making basket.
4. Moses' sister hiding him.
5. Moses being found by Pharaoh's daughter.
6. Miriam offering to find nurse.
7. Miriam returning baby to mother.
8. Miriam and mother thanking God.

Practice behind the screen until kids can change scenes quickly. Make certain shadows are clear and that all props can be seen. ■

—ML

## THINGS YOU'LL NEED:
☐ bed sheet
☐ spotlight or lamp
☐ *The Picture Bible*
☐ props

# Kids on
# *VIDEOTAPE*

**by Eric Thurman and
Judy Couchman**

Why not make a videotape of your "Joseph Special" or another dramatic presentation?

## FINDING EQUIPMENT
You don't have to buy thousands of dollars worth of technology to produce a decent videotape. Equipment usually can be borrowed or inexpensively rented from people in your church or community. You'll need:

**1. Camera.** In many churches, there's at least one person who owns a home video camera—so check for a camera to borrow in your congregation. If none is available, rent one from a home video store for about $20 to $25 per day. (Stay away from industrial or broadcast rental shops; they're more expensive.)

If there's a cable TV company in your city, see whether you can borrow a camera through the firm's public access department, which may loan equipment to the public for free. The cable system's loan program might also offer free instruction, simple editing, and even airing on one of its channels. Using equipment from a cable company may be more difficult and time-consuming than going with "home-style" video, however.

**2. Recorder.** Most home video recorders have a VHS format. But there's also Betamax, 8mm, and the ¼ inch used by professional camera crews. Borrow or rent whatever's convenient and available.

**3. Videotape.** Buy a new, brand-name tape instead of a used or off-brand discount type. The fresh tape

will have fewer "dropouts"—flashes that appear in a recorded picture.

**4. Microphone and extension cord.** A hand-held or clip-on microphone generally produces the clearest sound. A microphone extension cord will help you collect sound closer to the action, producing a clearer recording. Hold the mike no more than six inches from a speaker's mouth. If you can't borrow a mike and cord, they can be purchased for a reasonable price at an electronics stores.

**Idea:** If you've borrowed your camera and purchased a mike and cord, give them to the person who loaned you the camera. The gift will help express your thanks.

## ORGANIZING A CREW
Organize the production crew according to your kids' talents. If the group is large, assign one or more kids to every position. If it's small, each child may play several roles. It's best to combine positions that require similar abilities or can be logically handled together (i.e., producer/director; audio technician/grip). Your crew can include:

**1. Location scout.** Before the "shoot," this person selects the best location(s) for taping. Scouting a location involves checking for visual and audio distractions, good lighting, and best shooting angles. The scout also decides how to arrange the props and on-camera people—all before the crew and "actors" arrive.

If you're taping at more than one setting, the scout should always be one location ahead of the cast and crew. When designating this person, pick someone who loves detail, thinks ahead, and is punctual.

**THINGS
YOU'LL
NEED:**
- [ ] **videotape**
- [ ] **videotape camera**
- [ ] **videotape recorder**
- [ ] **microphone and chord**
- [ ] **lights**
- [ ] **crew**
- [ ] **actors**
- [ ] **script (You might use one from this book.)**

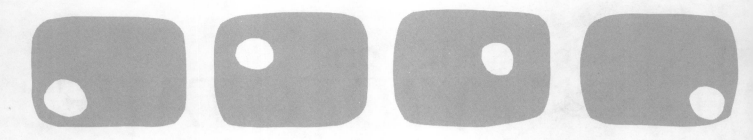

**2. Producer.** This crew member oversees the entire project. He or she develops the videotape's theme, sequencing, and production schedule, works with a writer to develop the script, and communicates the project's purpose to other crew members. The producer is a leader and a detail person who likes to take charge and motivate others to work.

**3. Scriptwriter.** Naturally, the writer should be a creative and perceptive person, able to capture an easy-to-read, conversational style in the script. He or she must work well with the producer and be comfortable gathering information from church families during preproduction interviews.

**4. On-camera host/hostess.** Conduct screen tests to determine the best host or hostess for your videotape. This teen will interview the featured families, so on-camera poise is crucial. The host or hostess should put others at ease, too.

Run tests a few days before production so the selected person can practice introducing the program and asking questions. To use all available talent, consider having several interviewers—perhaps one for each featured family.

**5. Director.** On the day of your shoot, a director accomplishes the producer's game plan. He or she arranges the subjects and directs their actions (called blocking), interprets the script, and leads the camera crew. The director is a motivator, able to bring out the best in others.

**6. Camera operator.** Try for someone who's already operated a home video camera. In addition to a steady hand (the people should move, not the equipment), the camera operator needs to fulfill the director's commands.

**7. Video operator.** This person starts and stops the video recorder, keeps its batteries charged, and if there's a TV monitor, checks to see that the picture coming from the camera looks correct.

**8. Audio technician.** The audio technician places the microphone(s), monitors the audio quality by keeping the needle out of the red area on the recorder's meter, and listens for sound interference. A good technician also conceals equipment cables and microphone cords so they aren't seen in the picture. (A clip-on mike, for example, can be attached to a collar with the cord running down the person's back.)

**9. Grip.** A service-oriented person, the grip carries equipment, speeding setup and strike (takedown) at each location. ■

—adapted from *Give It Away!* a volume in the Pacesetter series, ©1987, David C. Cook Publishing

# The 23rd Psalm Chant

**THINGS YOU'LL NEED:**
- [ ] at least eight copies of the script

**by Karen Burton Mains**

This dramatic choral reading weaves verses from Old and New Testaments to proclaim the love of the divine Shepherd. It can be presented by older children or teens (or a combination of the two). It would be especially appropriate for a worship service.

## READERS:
- [ ] Christ
- [ ] Psalm 23 (Four or more readers in *sotto voce*, a stage whisper which is hushed but loud enough for the audience to hear)
- [ ] Readers (Two or more)
- [ ] Voice 1
- [ ] Voice 2
- [ ] Choir (One person leading the chant which consists of three lines from Psalm 23, each with three beats. Be sure to emphasize the last beat of each line:

You are *my*
Shepherd *I*
Shall not *want.*)

If you use children, consider adding visual drama. Have children paint or color large, simple posters illustrating some of the lines. Children can hold up posters at appropriate points in the chant. That way the audience will enjoy both the chant and the children's artistic interpretations.

## PSALM CHANT

**Christ:** Truly, I am the Good Shepherd.

**Psalm 23:** The Lord is my shepherd; I shall not want.

**Chant:** You are *my*—Shepherd *I*—shall not *want*—

**Christ** *(Child 1 holds up poster illustrating the following lines)*: My sheep recognize my voice, and I know them, and they follow me. *(poster down)*

**Psalm 23:** He maketh me to lie down in green pastures: he leadeth me beside the still waters.

**Chant:** You are *my*—Shepherd *I*—shall not *want.*

**Christ:** If you had just one sheep, and it fell into a well on the Sabbath, would you work to rescue it that day? Of course, you would. And how much more valuable is a person than a sheep!

**Psalm 23:** He restoreth my soul.

**Chant:** You are *my*—Shepherd *I*—shall not *want.*

**Christ** *(Child 2 holds up poster illustrating the following lines)*: If you had a hundred sheep and one of them strayed away and was lost in the wilderness, wouldn't you leave the ninety-nine others to go and search for the lost one until you found it? And then you would joyfully carry it home on your shoulders. When you arrived you would call together your friends and neighbors to rejoice with you because your lost sheep was found. *(poster down)*

Well, in the same way Heaven will be happier over one lost sinner who returns to God than over ninety-nine others who haven't strayed away!

**Psalm 23:** He leadeth me in the paths of righteousness for his name's sake.

**Chant:** You are *my*—Shepherd *I*—shall not *want.*

**Christ** *(Child 3 holds up poster illustrating the following lines)*: Tonight you will all desert Me. For it is written in the Scriptures that God will smite the Shepherd, and the sheep of the flock will be scattered. I lay down My life for the sheep. *(poster down)*

**Psalm 23:** Though I walk through the valley of the shadow of death, I will fear no evil.

**Chant:** You are *my*—Shepherd *I*—shall not *want.*

**Christ** *(Child 4 holds up poster illustrating the following lines)*: And what pity I felt for the crowds that came, because their problems were so great and they didn't know what to do

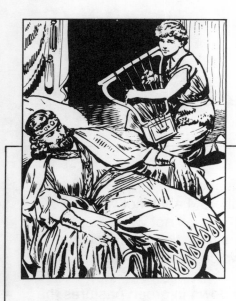

or where to go for help. They were like sheep without a shepherd. *(poster down)*

**Psalm 23:** For thou art with me; thy rod and thy staff they comfort me.

**Chant:** You are *my*—Shepherd *I*—shall not *want*.

**Christ:** I will feed My flock like a shepherd; I will carry the lambs in My arms and gently lead the ewes with young.

**Psalm 23** *(Child 5 holds up poster illustrating the following lines)*: Thou preparest a table before me in the presence of mine enemies: thou anointest my head with oil; my cup runneth over. *(poster down)*

**Chant:** You are *my*—Shepherd *I*—shall not *want*.

**Christ:** But when I, the Messiah, shall come in My glory, and all the angels with me, then I shall sit upon my throne of glory. And all the nations shall be gathered before Me. And I will separate the people as a shepherd separates the sheep from the goats, and place the sheep at My right hand, and the goats at My left. Then I, the King, shall say to those at My right, "Come, blessed of my Father, into the Kingdom prepared for you from the founding of the world."

**Psalm 23:** Surely goodness and mercy shall follow me all the days of my life: and I will dwell in the house of the Lord for ever.

**Chant:** You are *my*—Shepherd *I*—shall not *want*.

**Readers** *(Child 6 holds up poster illustrating the following lines)*: When the Head Shepherd comes, your reward will be a never-ending share in His glory and honor. *(poster down)*

**Readers:** And now may the God of peace, who brought again from the dead our Lord Jesus, equip you with all you need for doing His will. May He who became the great Shepherd of the sheep by an everlasting agreement between God and you, signed with His blood, produce in you through the power of Christ all that is pleasing to Him. To Him be glory forever and ever. Amen.

**Chant:** You are *my*—Shepherd *I*—shall not *want*.

**PRAISE PRAYER**

*(In the praise prayer, the choral choir will clap first and then chant: "You, O Lord, shepherd me." Consider having someone play the piano, guitar, or other instrument while this pastoral prayer is being presented.)*

*(Hold up same posters as before, one at a time, until all are held up.)*

**Voice 1:** Out from desolate pits.

**Chant** *(clap)*: You, O Lord, shepherd me.

**Voice 1:** Up from the miry bogs,

**Chant** *(clap)*: You, O Lord, shepherd me.

**Voice 1:** Set my feet on a rock,

**Chant** *(clap)*: You, O Lord, shepherd me.

**Voice 1:** Please make my steps secure,

**Chant** *(clap)*: You, O Lord, shepherd me.

**Voice 2:** Make me to know Your ways.

O Lord, teach me Your paths.

Lead me in the walk of righteousness.

Lead us like sheep.

Guide us like a shepherd guides a flock.

**Chant** *(clap)*: You, O Lord, shepherd me.

**Voice 1:** Out from desolate pits.

**Chant** *(clap)*: You, O Lord, shepherd me.

**Voice 1:** Up from the miry bogs,

**Chant** *(clap)*: You, O Lord, shepherd me.

**Voice 1:** Set my feet on a rock,

**Chant** *(clap)*: You, O Lord, shepherd me.

**Voice 1:** Please make my steps secure,

**Chant** *(clap)*: You, O Lord, shepherd me.

**Voice 2:** Make me to know Your ways.

O Lord, teach me Your paths.

Lead me in the walk of righteousness.

Lead us like sheep.

Guide us like a shepherd guides a flock.

**Chant** *(clap)*: You, O Lord, shepherd me. *(all posters down)*

*(The Praise Prayer is repeated twice.)* ∎

# CHILDREN'S HOME

## An Allegorical Christmas Play

**By Eric Potter**

This allegorical play can be performed by kids during the Christmas season.

**Staging:**

The play can be performed on a regular stage or in a church auditorium. Chorus should stand (and sit) in choir loft if it's in front of the church, otherwise to the right or the left of the stage. Stage left should lead to "other" parts of the orphanage and stage right lead "outside."

**Costuming:**

Orphans should wear old ragged clothes, mess up their hair, and smudge their faces—they'll love it. Policemen should wear blue if possible and maybe a badge made from cardboard and foil. The chorus may want to dress as orphans or in matching outfits (i.e., navy blue skirts and trousers, and white shirts).

**Props:**

You can use many or few, depending on your resources. A number of low tables could be used both for the dining room scene, and as beds for the night scene. Governor Good needs a wrapped Christmas present and a cane. You will also need a sign for the orphanage. A whip for Mister Fiend would add an effective touch.

**Cast:**

You should use older kids for Mister Fiend, Governor Good, Maria, and Joe. Bethel should be young. The chorus can be as big or small as you want. If you are low on actors you can cut the henchmen and policemen by one and have orphans double up on bit parts.

**MISTER FIEND**—director of the orphanage
**GOVERNOR GOOD**—the hero
**MARIA**—older orphan girl
**JOE**—older orphan boy—friends with Maria
**BETHEL**—young orphan girl
**JUDY**—older orphan girl
**MISTER FIEND'S HENCHMEN I, II, III** (use 2 girls, 1 boy)
**POLICEMEN** (use 2 girls)
**ORPHANS** (Around 10 including Joe, Maria, Judy, and Bethel. Some have small speaking parts.)
**CHORUS**—must be able to sing and recite together
**STAGE HANDS**—some kids may prefer making scene adjustments and doing lighting and sound.

You will need at least eight copies of the script.

## SCENE 1

**Setting:** dining room with side entrance (stage right), low tables. A sign by the side door says: "Wanderers Orphanage, Mister Fiend, Director."

*(Before lights come on,* Chorus *begins singing "I'm Just a Poor, Wayfaring Stranger" [available in* Hymns for the Living Church, *1974]. Sing first verse using the line: "I'm going there to see my mother." During second verse lights come on, children are sweeping and scrubbing floor, some are setting tables, others cooking, some carrying in wood, and others shoveling the sidewalk. In the second verse, chorus should sing the line: "I'm going there to see my father." Chorus stops singing. Orphans continue working for a few moments in silence.)*

**Chorus:** The sun rises and sets and rises and sets. We eat and work and sleep and eat and work and sleep. We are tired and we want to stop, tired, we want to stop, want to stop. Because everything seems empty.
*(Older boys begin chanting):* Empty, empty, empty, empty . . .
*(Girls and younger boys say the following part):* Mean Mister Fiend treats us like slaves. *(Shout the next part and pause between each phrase.)* Sweep the floor. Scrub the clothes. Chop wood. Shovel snow.
*(All):* We want to stop.

*(Enter, from stage left, Joe and another boy carrying a small Christmas tree. Children stop working and gather around tree. Boys set it up in the corner.)*

**Joe** *(excited)*: It's Christmas Eve! Let's decorate the tree.

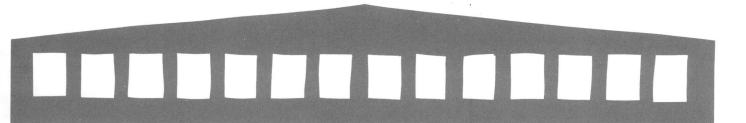

*(Kids cheer and begin decorating tree, all except Judy who sneaks off unnoticed. Enter Mr. Fiend and Henchmen led by Judy.)*

**Judy:** Over there. *(Points to kids around tree.)*

**Fiend:** What's the meaning of this? Why aren't you working? And what is that thing? *(Points to tree.)*

**Joe:** It's a Christmas tree, sir. Today's Christmas Eve, and . . .

**Fiend:** Quiet! Don't ever use that word here. *(to Henchmen 2 and 3)* Get rid of that branch. *(to Henchman 1)* Bring him with me. *(Points at Joe.)* The rest of you, get back to work. *(Kicks at a kid.)*

*(Fiend and Henchmen exit stage left dragging Joe by arm. Children resume work.)*

**CHORUS** *(Boys resume work chant. Others say)*: Poor, poor Joe, where did he go? The Fiend will box his ears.

## SCENE TWO
**Setting:** dining room, kids are milling around. Joe's head is bandaged.

*(A bell rings. Kids hurry to their seats. Henchman 1 enters from stage left and addresses the orphans.)*

**Henchman 1:** Silence! *(with sneering sarcasm)* What would you little dears like for supper? *(The following items called out by various orphans):* Chocolate chip cookies! Pizza! Ice cream! Tacos! Apple pie!

**Henchman 1:** Well, you can't have them. You get liver. *(Groans from orphans.)* Now get in line.

*(Makes first kid in line serve food. Judy should be close to the end of the line.*

*Chorus speaks as kids go through the line.)*

**Chorus:** We hate liver. We hate liver. We have it for breakfast. We have it for lunch. We have it for supper. Every day, every week, every year. Liver—yech!

*(Henchman stops line when it's Judy's turn.)*

**Henchman 1:** Are you the one that told on the other children?

**Judy** *(frightened)*: Yes.

**Henchman 1:** Then you don't have to eat this slop. Your reward is to dine with Mr. Fiend himself. He'll give you all the spaghetti and soda pop and chocolate cake that you can eat.

*(Exit stage left, Henchman and Judy. Rest of children finish through line. Lights go down.)*

## SCENE THREE
**Setting:** dormitory room (tables become kids' beds). Lights should be dim.

*(All the children are lying down except Maria and Joe who talk quietly.)*

**Maria:** Does your head hurt a lot, Joe?

**Joe:** Some, but it's not too bad.

**Maria:** I wish we could get away.

**Joe:** Me, too. But we can't. Believe me, I tried before.

**Maria:** What happened?

**Joe:** Nothing. I ended up back here. They found me and brought me back.

**Marie:** Where'd you go?

**Joe:** I ran through the woods till I came to the edge of a cliff. There was a stream running through the canyon. I could see fields on the other side, green fields with white dots. I thought I saw people walking around between the dots, so I shouted hello but no one ever answered.

*(Maria lets out a huge yawn.)*

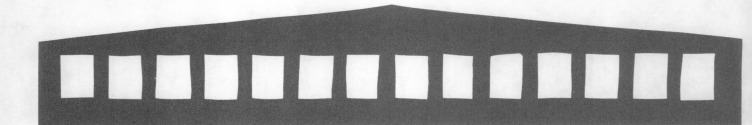

**Joe:** I guess we'd better go to sleep.

**Marie:** Yeah, maybe we'll be lucky and have good dreams.

**Joe:** What do you dream about?

**Marie:** I'm not sure. A face sometimes.

**Joe:** What kind of face?

**Marie:** I think it's a mother's face. I don't know what a mother looks like, but I think it's my mother.

*(Silence.)*

Oh, well, good night, Joe.

**Joe:** Good night, Maria.

*(They lie down.)*

**Chorus:** The orphans slip into a troubled sleep. They cry and shout at bad dreams. Their restless night noises rise like smoke from a fire.

*(Sing first verse of ''O Come, O Come Emmanuel.'' A young child begins crying. Maria wakes up and goes and kneels beside Bethel's bed.)*

**Maria:** What's wrong, Bethel?

**Bethel:** I had a dream.

**Maria:** A bad dream?

**Bethel** *(Shakes her head no)*: A good dream, about a man with a happy face and a big house with dogs and cats and a big Christmas tree, bigger than the man.

**Maria:** But why are you crying if it was a happy dream?

**Bethel:** Because I woke up here.

*(Maria puts her back to sleep. Enter Henchman 2 with flashlight. Walks around shining light like a prison guard.)*

**SCENE FOUR**

**Setting:** empty cafeteria, bright sunlight.

**Chorus:** It's Christmas morning but just another day at Wanderers Orphanage. Or is it?

*(Enter from stage left, Mr. Fiend and his henchmen. They stop at center stage and talk together silently. Someone knocks on the door. Fiend and friends keep talking. The person knocks louder. The center group stops. Someone knocks again.)*

**Fiend:** Well, get the door.

*(Henchman 3 answers the door. Good steps in boldly, carrying a large present under one arm.)*

**Good** *(in booming voice)*: Good morning and Merry Christmas! I'm Governor Good. *(Holds out his hand, but Fiend won't shake it)*

**Fiend** *(suspiciously)*: What's that? *(Nods toward present.)*

**Good:** It's a Christmas *(Fiend covers his ears at the word.)* present for the orphans.

**Fiend:** Fine, fine, we'll take care of it. *(Takes package from Good who hesitates to give it up. Fiend hands it to Henchman 2 and addresses him privately with his back to Good, so Good ''can't'' hear him.)* Here, put this little prize somewhere safe where those grubby brats can't get to it.

*(Exit Henchman 2, stage left. Fiend continues talking silently to his other henchmen. Then he notices that Good is still there.)*

**Fiend** *(rudely)*: What are you still hanging around for?

**Good:** Mind if I look around a bit? I grew up here, you know. I'm surprised you don't remember me.

**Fiend** *(looks hard at Good)*: Well, I don't. *(Looks straight at audience and confides.)* Orphans all look the same anyway. *(Turns back to Good and shrugs his shoulders.)* Suit yourself. Good day.

*(Exit Good stage right. Fiend and henchmen exit stage left.)*

*(Enter all orphans with work tools. Bethel and Maria on stage left. Maria is sweeping, and Bethel is holding dustpan.)*

**Chorus** *(chant)*: Empty, empty, empty, empty . . .

*(Enter Good from stage right. He stops and looks around. Children stop work and stare. Chorus stops chant. Only Maria keeps sweeping. Bethel is dangling dustpan at side and pointing at Good.)*

**Maria:** Come on, Bethel, pay attention. *(Sweeps a little.)* Bethel! *(Maria looks up at Bethel and then to where she's pointing.)*

**Bethel:** It's him.

**Maria:** Who?

**Bethel:** The happy face man in my dream.

**Good:** Merry Christmas, children! *(They stare blankly.)* But look at you! You're working on Christmas. *(Good looks around in unbelief. Joe steps forward, curious but also protective.)*

**Joe** *(pause)*: Who are you? And what do you want?

**Good:** I'm called Governor Good. *(with determination)* Someone's got to do something about all this.

**Maria:** But who, and what can they do?

**Good:** I'll tell you who—me. And as for what—why, I'll adopt you.

**Orphan 1:** What's adopt?

**Good:** It means that I'm taking you to live with me in my house.

**Orphan 2:** Is it as big as here?

**Good:** Bigger. It's a mansion with lots of rooms.

**Bethel:** And do you have dogs and cats?

**Good** *(to Bethel)*: Lots of them.

*(Orphans all start to cheer and clap. Enter Fiend and Henchmen from stage left. Children see them and stop cheering.)*

**Fiend:** What in Heaven's name is going on in here?

**Good:** I'm adopting these children.

**Fiend:** Impossible . . . You can't . . . Impossible.

**Good:** But I'm going to.

**Fiend** *(stands directly in front of Good)*: You can't, I said. They're mine! Mine! I own them!

**Good:** You don't own anybody. I'm taking them home and you can't stop me.

*(Fiend stomps on Good's foot. Good yells in pain and hops up and down on his other foot.)*

**Fiend:** Now get out of here before I get your other foot. *(Good grabs his cane and hits Fiend on the head. Fiend falls to floor. Good threatens henchmen with cane. They crouch around Fiend.)*

**Good:** Someone call the police.

*(Exit stage left one orphan. Sound of sirens. Police enter stage right.)*

**Policeman 1** *(doesn't see Good)*: Okay, what seems to be the problem here? *(Sees Fiend.)* Hey, what in the world . . . *(Looks at kids suspiciously.)* Who's responsible for this? *(Points at Fiend.)*

**Good** *(steps up from background)*: I am.

**Policeman 1:** Oh, Governor Good. Sorry, I didn't see you. What should I do?

**Good** *(pointing at Fiend and helpers)*: Take Mr. Fiend and his henchmen and throw them in jail. Then throw away the key.

*(Exit stage right policemen dragging Fiend and crowd. Fiend clutching head.)*

**Good** *(dusting off his hands)*: Well, that's settled.

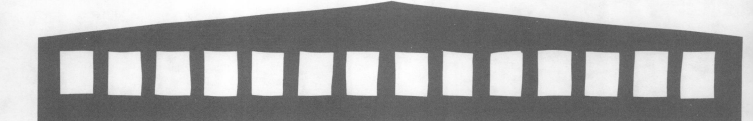

*(Good turns to leave.)*

**Maria:** Wait, aren't we coming with you?

**Good:** Not right now. I have to get things ready. But don't worry, I'm sending my limousine to pick you up. It will be here before dark.

**Chorus:** *(Sing first verse of "Joy to the World.")*

## SCENE FIVE

**Setting:** late afternoon, stage dim but not dark. Orphans (except Bethel) sitting around bored and sad.

*(Chorus sings "I'm Just a Poor, Wayfaring Stranger." This time use the line: "I'm going there to see my Savior.")*

**Orphan 1:** I'm hungry.

**Orphan 2:** Me, too.

**Orphan 3:** I don't think he's coming back.

**Maria:** Of course, he is. *(pause, then doubtfully)* He promised.

**Joe:** He's got to.

*(Enter Bethel from stage left, dragging Good's cane.)*

**Maria:** Hey, what is that, Bethel?

**Bethel:** It's his.

**Joe:** Whose?

**Bethel:** The man's.

**Maria:** The governor's cane! He left it.

**Joe:** Then he is coming. If he left his cane he has to come.

*(Sound of a horn honking.)*

**Orphan 4** *(stage right on tiptoes as if looking out a window)*: He's here.

**Chorus:** *(Sing first verse of "O Come, All Ye Faithful." Orphans should sing with the chorus and exit stage right one by one. As song ends, slowly dim the lights.)* ■

# III.

# BIBLE TIME PROJECTS

# MAKE A
# Relief Map

**THINGS YOU'LL NEED:**
- [ ] **bucket of fine sand**
- [ ] **aluminum baking pan or tub (the bigger, the better)**
- [ ] **plaster of paris or patching plaster**
- [ ] **bowl**
- [ ] **large spoon**
- [ ] **tempera paint, brushes**
- [ ] **felt-tipped markers**
- [ ] **Bible atlas (or enclosed map)**

Make a relief map of the ancient Middle Eastern world. For a pattern, see page 51. On this map, you can show the travels of Abraham, Isaac, Jacob, and Joseph.

Check a Bible atlas (or use enclosed map) for Abraham's world. You will need a map that shows UR, HARAN, CANAAN, and EGYPT. If you use an atlas, be careful. Some maps show only some of the places where Abraham traveled. Find one that shows mountains, too.

Pour several inches of sand into the baking pan. Remember that your landscape will be only as high as the sand is deep.

Dampen sand. Then make *holes* for places where seas will be.

Mix the plaster using instructions on the package. If you don't have instructions, pour 3 cups of cold water into a bowl, and pour dry plaster into the bowl until it is as high as the water. Do not stir or you will have lumps. Instead, vibrate water with a spoon, and the water will slowly seep into the plaster. When the plaster looks like a milk shake, it is ready to pour. (You can make more plaster if you don't have enough.)

Spoon plaster onto the sand. Fill up holes first, and then cover the whole surface with plaster until it is one inch thick. Do not fill up the whole pan with plaster, or you may have a hard time getting the dry plaster map out of the pan.

Wait one hour or until the plaster is cool. It will heat up when it is getting hard. Then lift it out of the pan and rinse off the sand.

Use tempera paint to color in ground, rivers, lakes, and seas.

**Map Additions**

● As you study the lives of Abraham, Isaac, Jacob, and Joseph, draw lines to show where they traveled. Also write in the names of towns and cities they visited.

● Let students use a line of glue and a strip of yarn to trace the route the captives took from Judah to Babylon.

● As students read about the fall and captivity, have them place important characters or events at specific locations on the "build-on" map. They can trace or cut out the illustrations on pages 52, 53 of this book, color them, and tape them to the indicated locations on the map.

● Students can make stand-up figures by gluing pipe cleaners or toothpicks to the backs of the completed illustrations. Lay the map on a large tabletop and stick the figures into bits of modeling clay stuck on the correct map locations. ■

—LT and RK

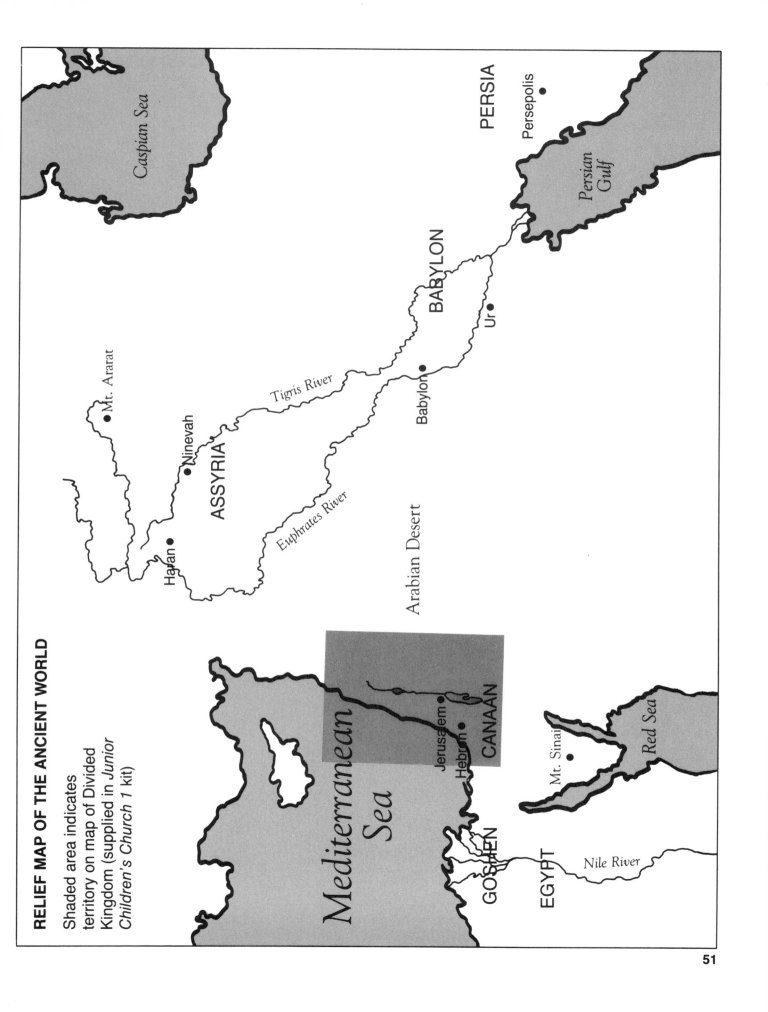

**RELIEF MAP OF THE ANCIENT WORLD**

Shaded area indicates
territory on map of Divided
Kingdom (supplied in *Junior
Children's Church 1* kit)

Caspian Sea

PERSIA

Persepolis

Persian
Gulf

BABYLON

Mt. Ararat

Ur

Tigris River

Ninevah

Babylon

ASSYRIA

Euphrates River

Haran

Arabian Desert

Mediterranean
Sea

Jerusalem

Hebron

CANAAN

Mt. Sinai

Red Sea

GOSHEN

EGYPT

Nile River

# ILLUSTRATIONS

**JERUSALEM**
Isaiah is called to be God's prophet.

**JERUSALEM**
Jerusalem is burned by the Babylonians.

**NEAR JERUSALEM**
Jeremiah sees a vision of destruction.

**BABYLON**
The beautiful hanging gardens of Nebuchadnezzar.

**NEAR BABYLON**
**Ezekiel preaches to captives in Babylon.**

**BABYLON**
**Daniel in the lions' den.**

**BABYLON**
**Three men in the fiery furnace.**

**JERUSALEM**
**Captives return to rebuild Jerusalem.**

# BIBLE-TIME MEAL

**THINGS
YOU'LL
NEED:**

- [ ] **vinyl tablecloths, blankets, or table covering**
- [ ] **pitcher of water**
- [ ] **paper cups**
- [ ] **bowl of beef or lamb stew**
- [ ] **bowl of raisins, apricots, or grapes**
- [ ] **damp towels**

**OPTIONAL:**
- [ ] **beans and a loaf of bread**

Spread white paper covering, vinyl tablecloths, or blankets on the floor.

Send one of the girls to get a big pitcher or water while other students set paper cups and bowls of food on the floor covering. Explain that in Bible times people ate their meals sitting on the floor around a low platform or eating directly from a cloth-covered floor.

Before eating, all repeat together, "God, we thank You for this food. Amen."

What you serve at the meal depends on your facilities. No plates or utensils are needed for the meal. People ate from large common bowls with the fingers. If possible, have a bowl of beef or lamb stew or beans and a loaf of unsliced bread. As the loaf is passed around, students break off small pieces and dip them into the stew. The pieces of bread serve as spoons and are then eaten with the stew. Fingers should not be licked. Continue the meal by passing around a bowl of raisins, apricots, or grapes, after which several volunteer "servants" can come with damp towels for cleaning hands. Conclude with another prayer of thanks: "You are to be praised, Lord our God, King of the world, for causing food to grow in the earth. Amen." ∎

# **S**EDER MEAL

For centuries Jewish people have celebrated deliverance from Egyptian slavery with a seder meal. Why not celebrate Passover with your group?

Discuss with the group whether they would like to invite their parents. Or they might celebrate the meal in front of the entire Sunday school. Once a decision has been made, hand out copies of the directions. Have children sign their names beside items they might bring from home. Go over steps they will take in putting on the meal, and ask for volunteers to take speaking parts.

If you decide to demonstrate before a large group, inform parents of the date of the presentation, time, and responsibilities of the children.

### Unleavened bread

In a bowl mix 3 cups whole wheat flour and 1 1/3 cups water (add a little more water, if needed). Cover a cookie sheet with brown paper and sprinkle flour on it. Spread dough over paper as if you were making a pizza. Make holes all over dough with a fork. Bake at 375 degrees for 15 minutes. To turn over the dough, pick up brown paper and flip dough over on cookie sheet. Then throw away the paper. After 15 more minutes, take out unleavened bread. Cool before eating.

### Seder Meal

Set plates, bowls, cups, and other items on a table. Then follow these steps.

1. Light two candles. The Hebrews did this at sundown on the first evening of Passover. Have someone say the following prayer: "We praise You, O Lord our God, King of the

## THINGS YOU'LL NEED:

- [ ] **two candles**
- [ ] **basin of water**
- [ ] **small pitcher of salt water**
- [ ] **eggs (hard-boiled) in a bowl**
- [ ] **horseradish**
- [ ] **vegetables (parsley, celery, carrot sticks)**
- [ ] **apple**
- [ ] **nuts**
- [ ] **grape juice**
- [ ] **unleavened bread or saltine crackers (If you make unleavened bread, you will also need whole wheat flour, water, cookie sheet, brown paper, fork, oven.)**
- [ ] **plates, cups**
- [ ] **slips of paper**

Universe. You have made us holy by giving us Your Ten Commandments, and You have commanded us to light the festival candles."

2. Wash hands. Circulate around the table with a pitcher of water. Pour water over each child's hands into a basin. Explain that the Hebrews did this as a ceremony of cleansing.

3. Have a child pour grape juice into cups. Explain that the Hebrews served four cups of wine during the Passover meal. These cups reminded them of four of God's promises found in Exodus 6:6, 7. Have four children repeat the promises:

   a) **I will deliver you from the Egyptians;**
   b) **I will deliver you from slavery;**
   c) **I will save you from sin;**
   d) **I will make you my people and I will be your God.**

4. Sprinkle a little salt water over the foods on the table. Have someone explain that the salt water represents two things:

   a) **The tears of the Hebrews while they were slaves;**
   b) **The salty waters of the Red Sea.**

5. Pass around the eggs. Explain that they represent a thank offering for the new life of freedom.

6. Have children taste a little horseradish. Do they like it? Explain that this herb represents the bitterness of slavery as well as the bitter water that the Hebrews found in the wilderness.

7. Have everyone take some parsley, celery, and carrot sticks. Explain that these vegetables celebrate the Hebrews' spring harvest. They also serve as reminders that the Hebrews were once slaves who grew crops.

8. Mix up chopped apple, nuts, and grape juice. Have everyone put a little on their plates. Explain that this mixture is called haroseth (huh-ROH-suth); it reminds the Hebrews of the clay mixture they used to make bricks for the Pharaoh. Dip bitter vegetables into haroseth to represent their suffering.

9. Hand around the matzo—unleavened bread, with many tiny holes in it. Explain that matzo is called the "Bread of Affliction." It represents the bread that was eaten hurriedly so that the Hebrews could quickly leave Egypt. (Use crackers if you don't have matzo.)

10. Have the youngest member of the Seder meal read each question below:

   **a. Why is this night different from all other nights? Why on this night do we eat only unleavened bread?** (Leaven is like modern yeast. It is thought to be impure because it ferments the dough. Any food burned as an offering to God did not have leaven in it.)

   **b. Why on other nights do we eat all kinds of herbs? Why on this night do we eat bitter herbs?** (Because the bitter herbs represent the bitter bondage that the Hebrews suffered as slaves in Egypt.)

   **c. Why on this night do we dip herbs in salt water and haroseth?** (Because the salt water represents the tears of the Hebrews who were slaves and the waters of the Red Sea. The haroseth stands for their suffering.)

   **d. Why on this night do we hold this Seder service?** (Have someone read Exodus 12:26, 27.) ∎

# Camp Around the
# *TABERNACLE*

**by Eve McNary**

## A Model Tabernacle

A good way to involve fathers in children's church is to enlist their help in building a model of the ancient Hebrew Tabernacle. Have them set up a tent, either indoors or outdoors. They can use a simple bed sheet to separate the Holy Place from the Holy of Holies. Wooden chests or cardboard boxes might represent the bronze altar, the altar of incense, and the Ark of the Covenant. A birdbath could serve as the laver. If a candle stand is available, use it to represent the Hebrew candlestick. To build the courtyard fence, laths can be stuck into the ground and white string can be tied from lath to lath. You might drape cloth over the laths if you have it.

## The Ancient Hebrew Tabernacle

The courtyard of the ancient Hebrew Tabernacle was about 150 feet long and 75 feet wide, half as big as a modern football field. The Tabernacle itself (into which only priests could go and above which rested God's cloud) was 15 feet wide and 45 feet long. Since there were about two million Hebrews when the Tabernacle was made, a big worship place was needed for them.

People usually came and went, rather than worshiping all at one time. They stood in the courtyard instead of being seated.

The Tabernacle was portable because the Hebrews were on the move through the desert. For 40 years they carried the Tabernacle from place to place with them. Finally in Canaan it was set up in Shiloh and

**THINGS
YOU'LL
NEED:**
- [ ] tent
- [ ] bed sheet

**OPTIONAL:**
- [ ] laths
- [ ] white string
- [ ] birdbath
- [ ] three wooden chests or cardboard boxes
- [ ] candle stand
- [ ] seven small loaves of bread

used many more years. When the Temple was erected in Jerusalem, the Tabernacle design was followed.

The Tabernacle had gold-covered furniture, elaborately embroidered curtains, fine linen cloth—the most precious things people owned. Everything was donated by God's people at Mt. Sinai.

## Have a Camp-out

Why not have a camp-out around the Tabernacle? Ask kids or entire families to bring sleeping bags and pretend to be the tribes of Israel in the wilderness. They might dress up in ancient Hebrew clothing (bathrobes, sandals, and scarves). They might also drink water from canteens; actually the Hebrews used gourds and animal skins to carry water.

When everyone has arrived, have them make tribal banners (see page 60 of this book for directions). Begin a march around the church, and have groups carry their tribal banners. As they travel, have them sing "My Deliverer," page 9 of *Worship Time Music Book,* and other rousing Hebrew songs.

At the end of the march, have the group gather in the courtyard of the Tabernacle and repeat the Ten Commandments together. You might also have someone dress up in a white robe to represent the High Priest. He could read the great commandment in Deuteronomy 6:4-9 and ask the people to promise to love God and obey all God's commands.

You might have some kids bake small loaves of bread and place them on the altar (dough is available in

supermarkets). Other kids might make manna (directions on page 59 of this book). Serve canned chicken to represent quail. ■

—LT

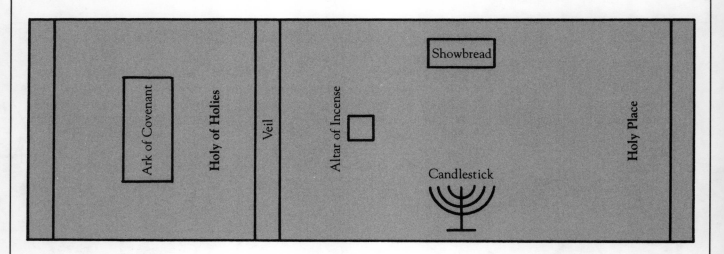

Courtyard of the Tabernacle

# MORTAR & PESTLE

**THINGS YOU'LL NEED:**
- [ ] **play dough recipe, page 67 of this book**
- [ ] **materials for play dough**

Bread making took up a lot of time for Palestinian women in Old Testament times. The rotary mill had not yet been invented, so corn or wheat had to be ground by hand to make flour. This was very hard work.

The tools used to grind flour were the mortar and pestle. The mortar was shaped like a bowl. The wheat or corn kernels were placed inside and then they were ground with the pestle.

Display copies of the picture below of a mortar and pestle and let your class make copies of them out of play dough. ■

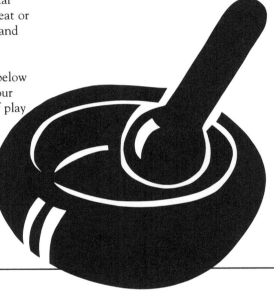

# *Brown Bread Recipe*

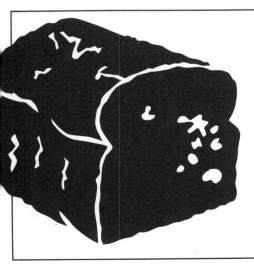

**THINGS YOU'LL NEED:**
- [ ] **¼ cup vegetable oil plus a little to grease pan**
- [ ] **½ cup molasses**
- [ ] **1 cup buttermilk (or milk with a little vinegar added)**
- [ ] **1 egg**
- [ ] **1½ teaspoons baking powder**
- [ ] **½ teaspoon baking soda**
- [ ] **1 teaspoon salt**
- [ ] **2 cups wheat flour**

Preheat the over to 350 F. Show a child how to grease 7 by 11-inch pan.

Ask one or more children to measure and mix flour, salt, baking powder, and salt.

Ask another child to measure and mix together buttermilk (or sour milk), molasses, oil, and egg.

Have a child add the liquid mixture to the flour mixture, and stir only enough to mix.

Pour batter into pan and bake for about 30 minutes. This recipe yields from 10 to 12 slices. ■

# THE FEAST OF *PURIM*

## THINGS YOU'LL NEED:

- [ ] **story of Esther, either using the play on page 34 of this book, or in the Bible**
- [ ] **noisemakers**
- [ ] **Bible-time costumes**
- [ ] **three-cornered pastry with filling inside (can be purchased at a bakery or grocery store)**
- [ ] **gifts for the poor (canned food, boxed cereal, etc.)**

When Queen Esther foiled the plot of the wicked Haman to kill all the Jews in Babylon/Persia, Mordecai was made prime minister in his place. Mordecai made a law that every year Jews should celebrate their deliverance in the Feast of Purim (meaning *lots*). Mordecai cast lots to decide when the Jews should be killed. Casting lots was something like tossing a coin for heads or tails.

The Feast of Purim is still celebrated by the Jews to this day on the fourteenth and fifteenth of the month of Adar (February or March), a month before the Passover.

Explain to your students the Jewish customs associated with this feast. Then have your own celebration.

Jewish customs for celebrating the Feast of Purim:

- [ ] There is always the retelling of the story in some form. The story might be read from Scripture, told in story form, or acted out as a drama.
- [ ] Every time Haman's name is mentioned, everyone boos or hisses.
- [ ] There are often noisemakers used at appropriate places throughout the story.
- [ ] Everyone dresses in costumes, as Esther, King Ahasuerus, Haman, or Mordecai. Props are simple: a moustache and beard, crown, scepter, shawl.
- [ ] Traditional food is a three-cornered pastry with filling inside, called "Hamantaschen," which means either "Haman's pockets," "Haman's hat," or "Haman's ear."
- [ ] Gifts are often taken to the poor.
- [ ] The general atmosphere is festive, with lots of noise, laughter, clapping, and cheering. ∎

—NJ

# Visit to a Jewish Synagogue

**THINGS YOU'LL NEED:**

- ☐ permission slips (provided below)
- ☐ synagogue in a your community
- ☐ means of transportation

Jews continue to celebrate the Passover and other Old Testament holy days.

Why not take your students to visit a synagogue for one of these occasions? The following Jewish holidays are special times to visit:

Passover—early April

Jewish New Year—September or early October

Yom Kippur (Day of Atonement)—early January

Hannukkah—late November or December

Purim—March

In advance, call a local synagogue and make arrangements for a tour of the building and possibly a visit to a worship service.

Before taking your students, visit the synagogue yourself so that you can prepare students for the experience. Explain to the rabbi or other leader that your students are exploring the Old Testament, and they would like to see firsthand how Jews continue to worship God on these holy days.

Ask if a rabbi or guide can explain the symbols and rituals to the children.

After arrangements have been made, copy a permission slip like the following, and be sure each student has it signed by a parent or guardian. Remind children about appropriate behavior on a field trip to a place of worship.

Have students write down some questions they might ask. Here are some ideas:

1. Look for the Star of David. How many points does it have? What is special about it?

2. Notice the platform in the synagogue. Usually there are two reading desks. What is their use?

3. The Ark of the Covenant should be at the back wall of the platform. What does this ark contain? (Often the rabbi will show the Torah kept in the ark.)

4. Look for the lamp which is usually near the ark. One name for it is the Eternal Light. What is it for?

5. Ask questions about the Hebrew worship service and music. Perhaps children will see prayer shawls and head coverings. Who wears these?

6. You will want to thank the rabbi for allowing the group to make the visit and answer questions. Who will do this? How will it be done? ■

**Field Trip Information**

To: _____

Date: _____

Leave church: _____

Transportation: _____

Detach and return by:

_____

I give permission for my child, _____ ,

to attend the field trip _____ ,

on _____ .

I hereby release the (specific church name) and individual drivers from liability in case of injury.

Signed _____

Phone _____

Date _____

# Jerusalem Market

The marketplace in ancient Jerusalem was a lively place—strings of untidy booths, caravans of merchants, beggars seeking coins, shopkeepers yelling about their wares or snoozing away the hours, and shoppers of every age and station in life.

You can help to create some of the flavor of Palestine in your classroom by setting up a craft display for parents with the theme of a Jerusalem market. Here are a few ideas to help with your display.

☐ Set up booths and even small tents along a hallway or around the walls of the classroom. Display crafts on brightly colored cloths in the various booths. Pottery, weaving, and other craft items from previous units may be gathered for display.

☐ Have the children dress in Palestinian costumes. Let some act as shopkeepers, some as shoppers, some as beggars.

☐ At one booth serve fresh bread that the children have made.

☐ Play Jewish folk music in the background.

☐ Invite the adults to walk through the Jerusalem market at the close of their worship service. This will be an excellent way for them to catch the spirit of what the children are learning in children's church. ■

—KL

# PALESTINIAN POTTERY

Let your students try their hand at pottery making. Below are several sketches of the types of pottery jars used by Palestinian Jews. The Israelites usually used a red clay that was taken from just below the surface of the soil. They used it to make pottery for everything from cooking to storing documents.

Provide modeling clay and let your students copy one of the examples below or create their own designs. In subsequent weeks, you may wish to bake the pottery and let the students paint designs on it. Display their finished work at the Jerusalem Market described on page 66 of this book. ■

—KL

## PLAY DOUGH RECIPE

### THINGS YOU'LL NEED:
- [ ] 1 cup flour
- [ ] 1 cup water
- [ ] ½ cup salt
- [ ] 2 teaspoons cream of tartar (Do not omit or dough will not stay fresh.)
- [ ] 1 tablespoon cooking oil
- [ ] food color
- [ ] oil of wintergreen or peppermint (available in drugstores.)

This recipe is so easy that the children can make it themselves. Bring in a hot plate or use the church kitchen.

Have children combine and mix all dry ingredients. Tell them to add water slowly, then oil, food color, and flavoring. Cook on medium heat until mixture forms a ball. When it is cool, have children knead it. Store in an airtight container and refrigerate for longer use. It keeps for months. ■

# IV.
# CRAFTS

# CREATION
## MAGAZINE

**THINGS YOU'LL NEED:**
- ☐ **18″ x 24″ newsprint and construction paper sheets**
- ☐ **a variety of magazines**
- ☐ **scissors**
- ☐ **rubber cement**
- ☐ **watercolor markers**

Have kids who love pictures make their own creation magazines. Fold big sheets of newsprint in half. Add a piece of construction paper or poster paper to make a cover for each magazine. Staple the seams, and you will have large magazines.

Help kids to think of God's Creation in fresh ways. On the chalkboard, list "Hot things God created," "Funny things God created," "Feelings God created," "Scary things God created." Ask kids to help you list other things they might like to include in their Creation magazines. List all suggestions. If you have a large group, divide them into smaller groups and let them decide which of the listed categories they want to include in their magazines. They might use a felt-tipped marker to label each page, and illustrate it with pictures from magazines or their own drawings.

On the last pages of their magazines, kids might picture their favorite things that God created.

Spend some time talking about the cover. Explain that designers think a long time about a magazine's cover. They want people to be interested in the contents. They also want to show what the magazine is all about. Help kids to select a title that shows what Creation was all about. They may want to paste pictures to the cover or make an abstract design.

When magazines are completed, display them in a prominent place. Encourage family members to look at them. The children might also show and explain them to a class of younger children. ■

—LT

# Animal Cracker Art

**THINGS YOU'LL NEED:**

- [ ] **animal crackers**
- [ ] **glue**
- [ ] **watercolors**
- [ ] **fingernail polish**
- [ ] **construction paper**
- [ ] **paper plates**
- [ ] **string**

Animal crackers and a little imagination can create a Noah's ark scene. This can be a fun project and a helpful reminder of Noah and the Flood.

Have children paint animal crackers with watercolors.

Let animals dry before coating them with clear fingernail polish. The polish will make them look glossy.

Children should make an ark out of construction paper and draw a background scene on a paper plate or construction paper. They may want to include Noah and his family. Glue ark and animals onto the background. Tape string to the back for hanging. ■

# WEAVE A SWATCH OF
# JOSEPH'S COAT

Have children fold one sheet of construction paper in half and draw a line about an inch from the open bottom edge. Then have them cut uneven lines down to the line they drew.

Others brightly colored sheets of construction paper should be cut into inch-wide strips nine inches long.

Have children weave these strips through the first sheet.

They can color designs on their "swatch," which may be somewhat like the material in the coat Joseph wore. ■

—ML

**THINGS YOU'LL NEED:**

☐ **sheets of different brightly colored construction paper (9″ x 12″)**
☐ **scissors**
☐ **pencil**
☐ **crayons or markers**

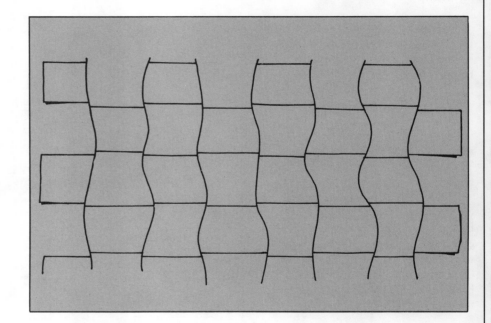

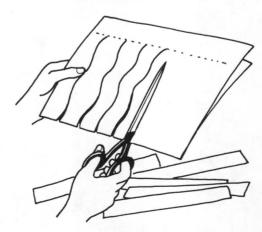

# MAKE A
# TANGRAM

In advance, cut a square of cardboard or construction paper as the diagram shows.

You will have five triangles, a rhomboid, and a square. Put a set in an envelope for each student.

The object of this activity is to arrange all seven pieces into a picture that shows a way God provides protection for us.

Have students glue their tangrams on pieces of construction paper. They can display them on a wall or bulletin board and explain what their tangrams represent. ■

—ML

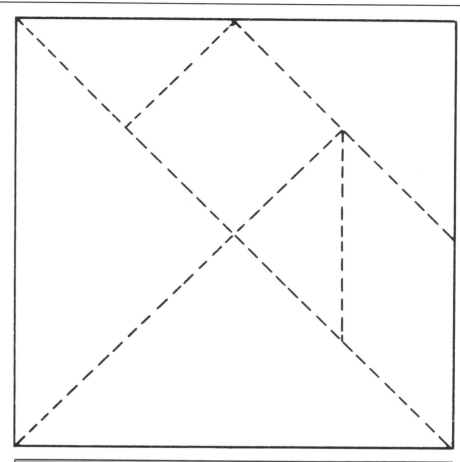

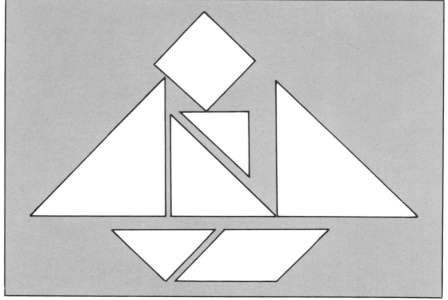

# BIBLE-TIME
# SCROLL

Have students pinch the end of one straw and stick it into the end of a second straw. They can do this with the second set of straws to make the ends of the scroll on which to roll the paper.

Next, have students remove the "tractor feed" holes from the sides of the computer paper. These strips of paper should be perforated and come right off.

Then have students tape the ends of the paper to the two long straws. Make sure the ends of the straw stick out evenly on either side.

When the paper is secured to the straws, ask kids to roll up the scroll and tie it with a piece of yarn. ■

—NJ

**THINGS YOU'LL NEED:**
- [ ] three sheets of computer paper (still attached), or tape three sheets of paper together
- [ ] four firm plastic straws (not flexi-straws)
- [ ] transparent tape
- [ ] yarn for tying and holding the rolled scroll

# BANNERS THAT PRAISE GOD

**THINGS YOU'LL NEED:**

- [ ] large felt pieces (12″ x 18″) for banner background
- [ ] felt scraps (many colors), lace, and other trim
- [ ] scissors, white glue
- [ ] dowel rods, ¼″ in diameter, 14″ long (or two inches longer than the width of the banner)
- [ ] a length of thick yarn, approximately 2′ long, for each banner

Have students fold over one end of the large felt piece (about 2½″ to 3″) and glue the end to the back of the banner.

Then have them cut out three half circles from the folded edge of the banner (as shown in the diagram), leaving four folded loops to hang the banner.

Show them how to insert the dowel through the loops, making sure the ends of the dowel stick out on either end about one inch.

Then have students tie the yarn to both ends of the dowel for hanging the banner.

Kids may decorate the banner background in any way they wish, using the scraps of felt to cut out letters, flowers, designs. They can use bits of lace and other trim to decorate their banner. They can glue all letters and decorations with white glue. ■

—NJ

For directions on other banners kids can make, see *Share the Gospel: Church Banner Patterns* and *Celebrate the Church: Church Banner Patterns* by Sandra Grant, David C. Cook Publishing Co.

**Design ideas:**

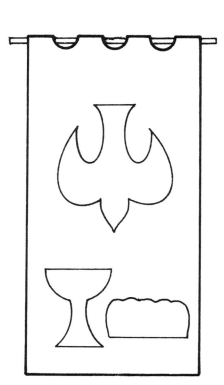

# Stained-Glass
# Window

Using the pattern on the next page, cut out the frame for the stained-glass window from construction paper.

Students may use the design on the pattern for the actual window cutouts, or they may design their own. (See alternative designs below.)

When the window design has been cut out, have kids tape or glue colored tissue paper or cellophane *behind* the cutouts.

Then they can fold the sides of the window forward so that the stained-glass window can stand on its own. ■

—NJ

**THINGS YOU'LL NEED:**

- [ ] one sheet of construction paper for each window
- [ ] stained-glass window pattern
- [ ] scissors, glue or tape
- [ ] different colors of thin tissue paper, or different colors of cellophane

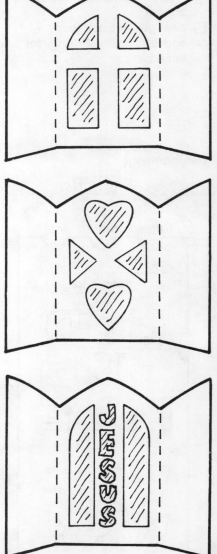

# Pattern for Stained-Glass

**Use black or colored
construction paper for
window frame**

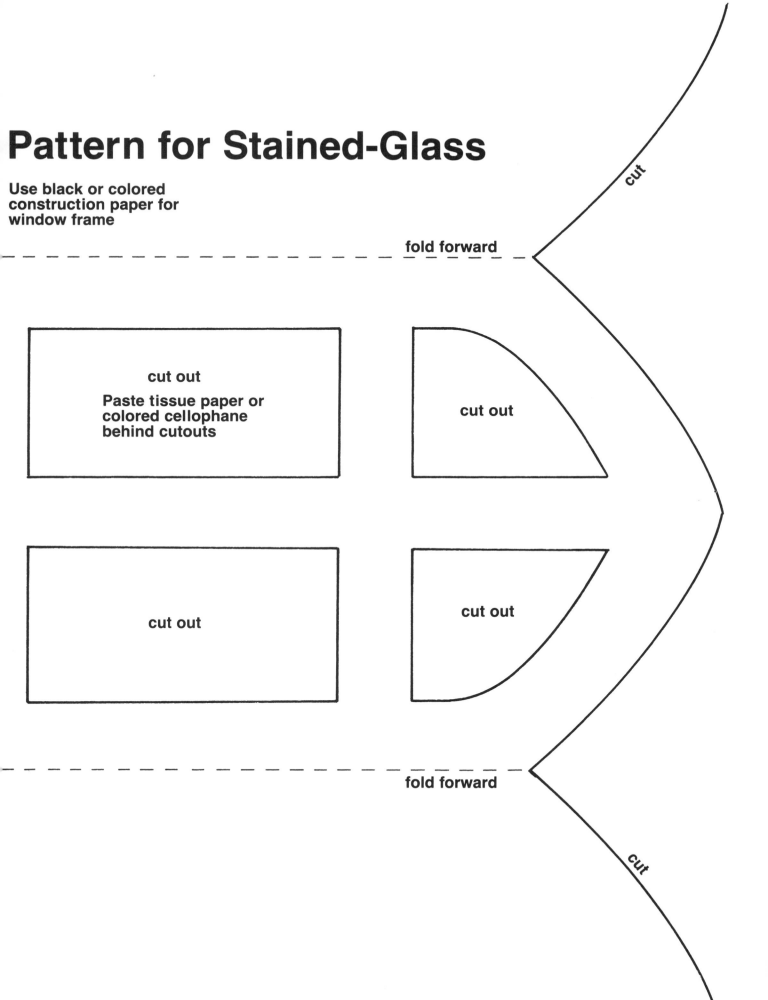

fold forward

cut out

**Paste tissue paper or
colored cellophane
behind cutouts**

cut out

cut out

cut out

fold forward

cut

cut

# Stand-up Benediction Card

**THINGS YOU'LL NEED:**
- [ ] green or blue construction paper
- [ ] red construction paper
- [ ] white construction paper hearts
- [ ] glue

Let kids make this card for themselves or someone they know.

1. Cut a piece of green or blue construction paper in half, lengthwise. Give half to a friend.

2. Fold the strip into three equal sections.

3. Fold back, in half, the two outside pages so their creases meet in the center.

4. Cut two smaller pieces of red paper the same size. Put these together, fold them carefully, and cut out a heart shape.

5. Glue the two hearts over the folded flaps, making sure that they come together as one heart when the flaps are closed.

6. Cut out a large white heart and glue it on the inside center of the card.

7. On the white heart, print a benediction to keep or give as a reminder of God's blessing. Select one such as Romans 15:5, Philippians 4:7, etc. ■

—RK

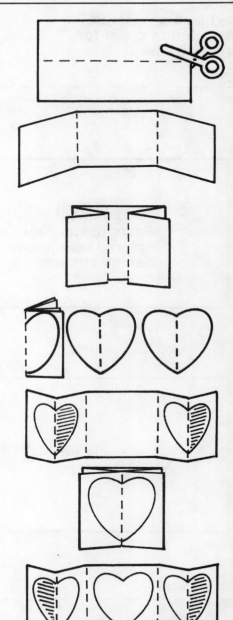

# BENEDICTIONS TO EAT

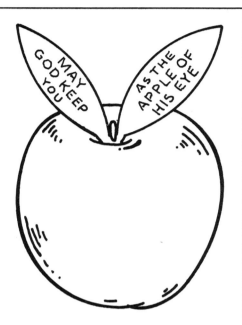

## THINGS YOU'LL NEED:
- [ ] apples, oranges, donuts
- [ ] green construction paper
- [ ] toothpicks
- [ ] felt-tipped marker
- [ ] glue or tape

Let students add blessings to apples, oranges, and doughnuts and give these as gifts to friends or relatives.

### APPLES
Cut leaf shapes out of green construction paper. Print a blessing on the leaves, and use a toothpick to attach them to an apple.
"May God keep you as the apple of His eye."

### ORANGES
Use a felt-tip marker to write a blessing around the outside of an orange: "Orange you glad to know God loves you?"

### DONUTS
Print a blessing on a slip of paper. Glue the paper to a toothpick, and stick the blessing flag into a donut. Blessing: "Donut forget: God is with you!" ■

—RK

# 'GET SMART' KID BOOKS

**THINGS YOU'LL NEED:**
- [ ] Bibles
- [ ] construction paper
- [ ] staples
- [ ] felt-tipped markers
- [ ] cardboard
- [ ] brightly colored adhesive-backed paper
- [ ] 17-inch pieces of yarn

King Solomon is sometimes said to be the wisest man who ever lived. Many of his wise sayings are found in the Book of Proverbs.

### Favorite Proverbs

Read through Proverbs, and select those that you think would be appropriate for the children in your class. Suggestions: Proverbs 13:20; 10:4; 15:1; 17:9; 11:12; 19:17; 3:5.

Explain to the children that much of the Book of Proverbs was written by the wisest man in the world. A "proverb" is a piece of good advice. List references from Proverbs on the board, and have kids look up verses and read them aloud. Discuss their meaning. Have the group help you write these proverbs in their own words. Try to keep paraphrases short.

### Kid Books

Give each child five sheets of white construction paper, and have them fold these in half widthwise. Explain that the first paper is their title page. They will write the title of the book and the author on it after they have completed the contents. Explain that they will print a proverb that they like at the bottom of each of four pages. Then they will illustrate each proverb on the rest of the page. After kids have completed their illustrations, have them help you make up their own "kid proverbs" on the chalkboard. Then have them select four to include in their books. Tell them to illustrate these sayings.

### Title Page

On the title page, have each child write a title, his or her name, name of the church, and date. You might show kids a sample title page from any book so that they understand why they are including this information

on the first page of their books. They will have a blank page at the back of their books.

### Book Covers

To give the books durability, have children make covers. In advance, make a sample book cover with adhesive-backed paper attached to it. This way, you will see what problems children may have finishing their covers.

If adhesive-backed paper is not available, simply use poster board covers.

Cut cardboard so that it is the same size as the construction paper booklets when they are folded flat. Fold each cardboard cover in half carefully so that its crease is smooth.

Cut pieces of brightly colored adhesive-backed paper so that they are ½-inch larger than the covers. To help children get the adhesive paper properly placed on their cardboard, show them that adhesive paper has a backing which must not be removed until the right time. Have them fold back a small part of the backing on the adhesive paper and line it up. Tell them to take the backing paper off a little at a time. Once the adhesive paper is lined up, then they pull off the backing and smooth the adhesive paper down on the book cover. Demonstrate so that they know what to do.

**Assembled Books**

Put the cover on the contents of each book. Punch two holes along the fold of each book near the bottom and top edges. Then have children open their books flat, put 17-inch pieces of yarn through the holes, and tie the yarn in a bow on the outside.

It takes a bit of time and effort to make sturdy children's books. But the kids will be so proud of them that they will treasure them for years.

## Don't make fun of others. If you're wise, you'll be quiet. Proverbs 11:12 ■

—LT

# V.
# LEARNING GAMES

# CONCENTRATION GAME

**by Karen Dockrey**

This game consists of two kinds of cards. One kind of card has one word, the name of a person, place, or thing from the story. The other kind of card has a phrase describing one of the words from the first set of cards. For example, one card might read "Rahab" and its companion card "The woman who hid Joshua's two spies."

To play the game, the children should turn the cards facedown. As each child takes a turn, he or she turns over two cards and checks to see if they match. One of the cards must be a single word and the other must be a phrase. The phrase must define the single word. If the cards match, the child keeps them and takes another turn. If cards don't match, the child returns them to their original spots and another player takes a turn. The children can refer to *The Picture Bible* if they are not sure if their cards match.

Photocopy and cut apart these cards. Give one card to each student. The numbers in parentheses indicate the page(s) in *The Picture Bible* where the object of each pair is found. Keep a copy of this sheet so that you can help the children find the right page should they have difficulty finding their matches. Make sure you cut the page numbers off the cards before you give them to the kids. ■

| Joshua 2-6 | |
|---|---|
| 174 <br> **HEBREW SPIES** | Hid on Rahab's roof in Jericho. |
| 174 <br> **RAHAB** | Believed that God would help the Israelites take over her home city of Jericho. |
| 175 <br> **TWO WALLS** | Protected Jericho from enemy soldiers. |
| 176 <br> **JORDAN RIVER** | Stopped flowing when the Hebrew priests began to cross it with the ark. |
| 177 <br> **12 STONES** | Reminded the Hebrews of how God had stopped the Jordan River so that the people could cross it. |
| 178 <br> **PASSOVER** | Feast the Hebrews celebrated when they entered the Promised Land. |
| 179 <br> **CAPTAIN OF THE LORD'S ARMY** | Told Joshua how to take Jericho. |

| 180 SEVEN PRIESTS | Marched around Jericho and blew trumpets on the seventh day. | 185 GOD | Told Joshua that the Israelites were being punished because someone had disobeyed God when the Israelite army had taken Jericho. |
|---|---|---|---|
| 181 GOD | Caused the walls of Jericho to fall flat. | 186 ACHAN | Admitted that he had sinned against God and his people. |
| JOSHUA | Told the Hebrew people how to destroy Jericho. | 187 ISRAELITE ARMY | Set fire to the city of Ai. |

## Joshua 6-24

| 182 JOSHUA | Said that no one was to keep anything from the city of Jericho when the army destroyed it. | 184 AI ARMY | Defeated the Israelites in the first battle. |
|---|---|---|---|

## Judges 1-13

| 183 ACHAN | Buried stolen treasure that he took from the city of Ai. | 195 DEBORAH | Judge of Israel who told the people God's plan for defeating the Canaanites. |
|---|---|---|---|
| 183 JERICHO | Was destroyed so that the Israelites would not copy its evil ways. | 195 BARAK | Leader of the Army that defeated the Canaanite army. |
| 184 JOSHUA'S SCOUTS | Discovered that the army of Ai was small. | 196 MUD | Trapped the chariots of the Canaanites. |

| 197 | | 204 | |
|---|---|---|---|
| **40 YEARS** | There was peace for this long and then the Israelites forgot God. | **TRUMPETS, PITCHERS, TORCHES** | Used by Gideon's army to defeat the Midianites. |

## Judges 13-16

| 198 | | 205 | |
|---|---|---|---|
| **BAAL** | The false god that the Israelites worshiped. | **PHILISTINES** | Attacked the Israelites and made their children slaves. |
| 198 **GRAIN** | Stolen from the Israelites by desert tribesmen and other enemies. | 205 **VOW** | Samson's mother made this to God when she promised never to cut his hair or give him strong drink. |
| 199 **GIDEON** | A farmer chosen by God to save Israel. | 206 **IRON SPEARS** | Weapons the Philistines had but the Israelites did not have. |
| 201 **WOOL** | Gideon asked for signs from God two times with this. Also called a "fleece." | 207 **SAMSON'S WIFE** | Philistine woman who did not worship God. |
| 202 **32,000** | The number of men Gideon first had in his army. | 208 **RIDDLE** | What Samson wanted the Philistines to answer or they would have to give him a reward. |
| 202 **300** | The number of men in Gideon's army that defeated the enemy. | 210 **30 ROBES** | Samson got these by killing 30 Philistines. |

| 212 | FOXES | What Samson used to destroy the Philistines' vineyards and fields of grain. |
| --- | --- | --- |
| 213 | JAWBONE | What Samson used to kill many Philistine soldiers. |

## Judges 16

| 219 | SEVEN BOWSTRINGS | Samson said that if he was tied up with these, he would lose his strength. |
| --- | --- | --- |
| 219 | DELILAH | A Philistine woman who tricked Samson. |
| 219 | 5500 SILVER PIECES | What Delilah was paid for finding out the secret of Samson's strength. |
| 220 | SLEEPING | What Samson was doing when his hair was cut. |
| 221 | SAMSON | Judge of Israel who was blinded. |

| 224 | TEMPLE OF DAGON | Where many Philistines were killed by Samson. |
| --- | --- | --- |
| 222 | GRAIN | What Samson had to grind when he was blind. |
| 224 | SAMSON'S STRENGTH | Given by God to deliver the Israelites from their enemies. |

# 'WISE IS RIGHT'
## GAME SHOW

**THINGS YOU'LL NEED:**
☐ chairs
☐ cue card

**OPTIONAL:**
☐ recorded game-show music
☐ tape recorder

In advance, print "CLAP" on a piece of construction paper. If possible, make a tape recording of the music of a TV game show. Cut apart the Question Cards printed below, and set chairs in front of the room.

When you are ready to begin, play the tape of game-show music. Then announce the "Wise Is Right" TV game show. Call four students' names and announce, "Come on down. You're the next contestants in the 'Wise Is Right' Game Show!" Hold up CLAP cue card and encourage kids to clap.

When contestants are in their places, read a hypothetical situation from a Question Card printed below. Then read the four possible solutions. The first contestant to stand and give an answer that reflects God's wisdom wins three points. If the contestant gives a good reason for this answer, he or she gets three more points. After several rounds of the game, total points and declare a winner.

Only five situations are provided, so think of many more on your own. If you wish, provide small prizes for correct answers. ■

**1** When Dick rides to church on Sunday morning, he shares the backseat with his sister Jenny and the baby. The baby sits in a car seat by one window. Dick always races to the car and sits by the other window. Jenny always whines, "I want the window." She keeps whining until Dad gets mad and yells. Then Jenny wails even louder. By the time the family gets to church, everyone is mad. If I were Dick, I would:

a. Give Jenny candy to keep her quiet.
b. Call Jenny a little brat.
c. Make Jenny go to church with another family.
d. Let Jenny sit by the window half the time.

**2** Sarah never seems to remember her homework assignments, so she gets into trouble with her teacher. Sarah has an assignment notebook to remind her of her assignments, but she leaves it at school. What should Sarah do to get her assignments done?

a. Keep her assignment notebook in her purse so she doesn't leave it at school.
b. Try to do well in class so that she can make up for the zeros she gets on homework assignments.
c. Copy homework assignments from someone else's paper.
d. Ask her mom to call the teacher every day and get the assignments.

**3** Tom wants a new ten-speed bike, but his dad says ten-speed bikes are too expensive. What should Tom do?

a. Keep begging his dad for a ten-speed bike.
b. Steal a ten-speed from a bicycle shop.
c. Borrow a friend's ten-speed bike whenever possible.
d. Offer to earn half the money for a ten-speed bike.

**4** Judy's mom is in the hospital, so Judy is stuck taking care of her two-year-old brother, Justin. The problem is that Justin has the flue and cries a lot. Judy would like to go for a walk in the park. What should she do?

a. Leave Justin at home in his crib and go to the park.
b. Take Justin next door and ask the neighbor to keep him.
c. Put Justin in his stroller and take him to the park.
d. Stay home and watch TV instead of going to the park.

**5** A new girl in Sunday school has invited Ellen to an overnight party. Ellen said she could go. Then Ellen found out that her friends don't like the new girl and they don't want to go to the party. They say that Ellen shouldn't hang around with that weird girl or she'll be weird, too. What should Ellen do?

a. Pretend to be sick and tell the new girl she can't go to the party.
b. Call her friends a bunch of creeps for being mean to the new girl.
c. Go to the party.
d. Tell the new girl to call off the party because nobody wants to go.

**6**

**7**

**8**

—KL

# BIBLE BASKETBALL

Each student should write three or more review questions. Shuffle these and pick questions at random.

The class divides into two teams. The teacher asks a tip-off question, and the first team to answer correctly gets the first chance to sink a basket.

Read the first game question to the team that answered the tip-off. If the team players answer without being blocked by the other team, they score two points. If they give no answer, they neither score nor lose points.

*Blocking:* After each answer, the teacher lets the opposition say if that answer is incorrect. If students say that it was incorrect, they have blocked the answer. If their accusation is correct, the other team does not score and the blocking team gets one point and an opportunity to correctly answer the question. If they give the right answer, they earn another point. If they give an incorrect answer, their score doesn't change. However, if they have incorrectly blocked and the answer given by the other team was correct, the blocking team fouls and loses two points.

If the original answer was incorrect but the opposing team does not block it, the teacher gives the correct answer and the team giving the incorrect answer is allowed to keep the two points it scored.

(Additional rule for advanced players: each team member must take his turn answering a question. No member may answer a second time until each player has answered once.)

A winning team is declared when time is up or when one team obtains a set number of points. ■

—from *Creative Teaching Methods* by Marlene LeFever, ©1985 David C. Cook Publishing Co.

# VI.
# INDIVIDUAL EXPRESSION

# GOD'S FAVORITE CREATION

You are God's favorite creation. Draw the funniest thing about yourself that most people don't know.

# AN ARCHEOLOGIST'S FINDINGS

You are an archeologist digging near Mt. Ararat. You are looking for tools and equipment that Noah used to build the ark. What might you find?

# ANIMALS IN THE ARK

Draw the inside of the ark.
Don't forget all the animals.

# HELP
# STAMP OUT
# FIGHTS

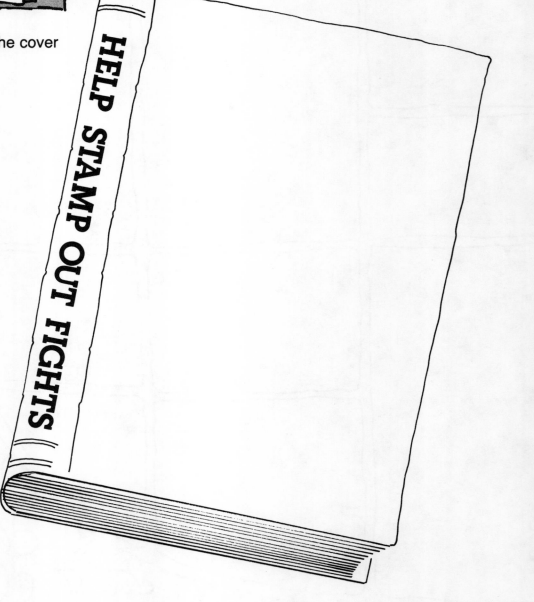

Make a picture for the cover of a new book.

HELP STAMP OUT FIGHTS

# PUT A MESSAGE IN GOD'S EAR

# GOD'S STRENGTH BOOKLET

Develop your physical and spiritual muscles by following these daily exercises!

Begin your exercise session by warming up your body. That way you will not strain a muscle. The first exercises listed below should be done slowly. Gradually exercise faster and faster.

1. **Jog in place.** Slowly jog in place, moving each foot from toe to heel. Swing your arms loosely. Jog three minutes. Feel loose and completely relaxed.

2. **Windmills.** Stand with your arms parallel to the floor, your legs apart. Bend from your waist and swing your right arm down to your left leg. Bounce twice at the bottom of swing. Try to keep your arms and body relaxed. Then bring your arm back up to the starting position. Do the same exercise with your left arm. Ten times in all. Then relax.

3. **Arm Stretches.** Put your feet together and raise your arms straight overhead. Slowly reach up, keeping your heels pressed together. Hold while you count five. Then slowly bring your arms down. Bend from your waist and keep your knees straight. Touch the floor with your fingertips. Hold while you count to five. Then return to your starting position. Repeat this five times.

4. **Arm Swings.** Stand with your knees and legs straight, your legs apart, and your arms relaxed at your sides. Slowly swing your arms forward, up over your head, back behind your body, and down and around to the front. Your arms should make a full circle.

5. **Leg Stretches.** Lift your right leg, toes pointed, straight out in front of you. Don't bend your knees. Lift your leg up and down rapidly ten times. Return to the starting position. Then do the same thing with your left leg. Do both legs ten times.

At the top of the grid put the names of exercises and leave space beneath for marking number of times kids did them. ■

# Week 1

God has given us many things that can help build up our faith muscles. One is found in each of the Scripture references below.

Each day read the verses and jot down one way you can use that piece of equipment to pass your next faith test.

Also keep track of the number of exercises you do.

| | | This column is for you to fill in according to each week's instructions. | Jog (min.) | Windmills | Arm Stretches | Arm Swings | Leg Stretches |
|---|---|---|---|---|---|---|---|
| M | MARK 11:24 | | | | | | |
| T | John 16:13 | | | | | | |
| W | Psalm 119:105 | | | | | | |
| T | Psalm 95:6 | | | | | | |
| F | Acts 16:25 | | | | | | |
| S | James 2:17, 18 | | | | | | |

## Week 2 Christians face a lot of tough situations. But God will give us powerful help to handle them.

Think of one area in your life that you struggle with. Read each day's verses as a prayer to God. Think of how these verses apply to your problem. Write down thoughts that pop into mind.

Also keep track of the number of exercises you do.

| | | This column is for you to fill in according to each week's instructions. | Jog (min.) | Windmills | Arm Stretches | Arm Swings | Leg Stretches |
|---|---|---|---|---|---|---|---|
| **M** | Psalm 31:1-4 | | | | | | |
| **T** | Psalm 27:1-3 | | | | | | |
| **W** | Psalm 34:17-19 | | | | | | |
| **T** | Psalm 94:17-19 | | | | | | |
| **F** | Psalm 91:1-6 | | | | | | |
| **S** | Psalm 28:6, 7 | | | | | | |

# Week 3

Each day tell the Lord about something hard you are facing. The more you turn to God, the stronger your faith becomes. Then look up an encouraging verse. Write down one word from the verse that reminds you that God will help you.

Also keep track of the number of exercises you do.

| | | This column is for you to fill in according to each week's instructions. | Jog (min.) | Windmills | Arm Stretches | Arm Swings | Leg Stretches |
|---|---|---|---|---|---|---|---|
| M | Psalm 3:4 | | | | | | |
| T | Psalm 34:4 | | | | | | |
| W | Lamentations 3:57 | | | | | | |
| T | John 14:13 | | | | | | |
| F | I Peter 5:7 | | | | | | |
| S | Matthew 7:7 | | | | | | |

# Week 4

You can develop your faith muscles by doing your daily exercises. Read these Scriptures and complete the following sentence each day. Also keep track of the number of exercises you do.

**Today, I will trust God for:**

| | | This column is for you to fill in according to each week's instructions. | Jog (min.) | Windmills | Arm Stretches | Arm Swings | Leg Stretches |
|---|---|---|---|---|---|---|---|
| **M** | Romans 5:12 | | | | | | |
| **T** | James 1:5, 6 | | | | | | |
| **W** | I John 3:23 | | | | | | |
| **T** | Ephesians 6:10, 11 | | | | | | |
| **F** | James 2:14-18 | | | | | | |
| **S** | John 5:24 | | | | | | |

# COAT OF ARMS

A coat of arms shows people who you are and what things are important to you. Create your own coat of arms.

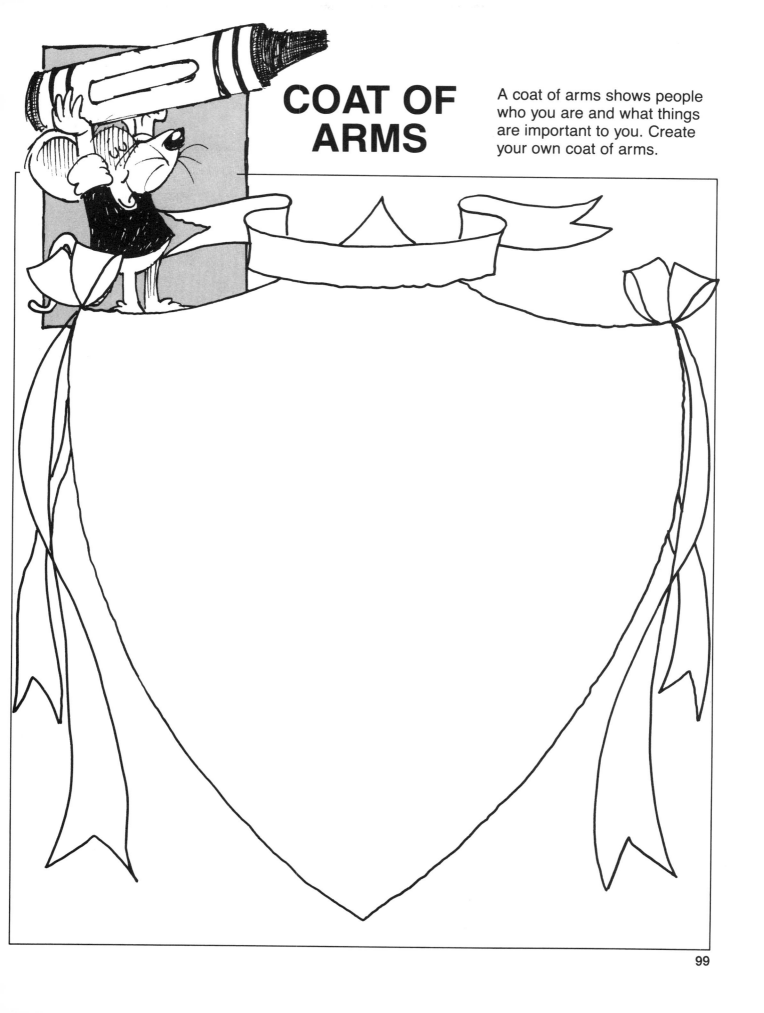

# THE SUNDAY

**You are going to be searching for God in your church. He's always there, of course, but sometimes we forget.**

Check the things in this list that make you forget that God really is in your church.

_____ I'm sleepy when I go to Sunday school and church.
_____ My friends laugh and talk so much that I can't listen.
_____ I don't understand what adults are saying about Jesus.
_____ I can't sit still for such a long time.
_____ I don't want to come.

If you go on the Sunday Search, you just might start saying things like:
- Sunday is so important that I'll go to bed earlier on Saturday. Then I won't be sleepy Sunday morning.
- I talked to my friends about the Sunday Search and they started searching, too. Now we all pay attention.
- I ask older Christians about stuff I don't understand.
- I get excited about church, and now I can sit longer.
- I want to go to church.

From *50 Days to Welcome Jesus to My Church*, a devotional study by David and Karen Mains with children's guide by Marlene LeFever used here. For additional information on this program for accelerated Christian growth, write The Chapel of the Air, Box 30, Wheaton, IL 60189.

# SEARCH

**Here are the rules for the Sunday Search.**

**Rule 1:** Go to church on Sunday morning, and look for one way God is speaking to you. He won't speak out loud. But He will let you know He is there and He is glad you came.
  Here are some ways God speaks to people in church.
  - The pastor or your teacher reads the Bible and you hear a message in the verses for you.
  - You sing a song and you think, "I'm really glad I love Jesus."
  - The pastor preaches and you know he is saying what God wants you to hear.

It's a funny thing. If you go to church expecting God to speak to you, He will. And you will know it!

**Rule 2:** Go to church, and look for one way God uses you to speak to others. Obviously God speaks through the lady who sings and the man who teaches. But He will also speak through you. Here are some ways God might have spoken through you to other people in your church.

Ways God Might Speak Through Me:

_____ I said good morning to someone who looked sad.
_____ I helped a mother get her baby to stop crying.
_____ I set up chairs and cleaned my Sunday school area.
_____ I saved a seat for a kid nobody likes.
_____ I said thank you to an usher.

You see! God can speak through you to other people. In this Sunday Search, you will discover seven ways He speaks through you on Sunday.

**Rule 3:** You must talk about Rule 1 and 2. Share with your family how God spoke to you and through you each Sunday. Why not talk on the way home from church or during the noon meal?

You are going to be pleased with what you discover. You'll also have fun listening to what your parents tell you about their Sunday Search. ■

# Going on the Sunday Search

Complete the following chart:

**1)** How Christ spoke **TO** me: _____
_____ .

How Christ used me to speak to **OTHERS**: _____
_____ .

I **TALKED ABOUT** what happened with: _____
_____ .

**2)** How Christ spoke **TO** me: _____
_____ .

How Christ used me to speak to **OTHERS**: _____
_____ .

I **TALKED ABOUT** what happened with: _____
_____ .

**3)** How Christ spoke **TO** me: _____
_____ .

How Christ used me to speak to **OTHERS**: _____
_____ .

I **TALKED ABOUT** what happened with: _____
_____ .

**4)** How Christ spoke **TO** me: _____
_____ .

How Christ used me to speak to **OTHERS**: _____

I **TALKED ABOUT** what happened with: _____
_____ .

# VII.
# BULLETIN BOARDS

ABCDE
FGHIJK
LMNO
PQRST

U V W X
Y Z a b c
d e f g h i
j k l m n o

pqrstu
vwxyz
12345
67890

# PRAYER
## BULLETIN BOARDS

**By Robert Klausmeier**

**THINGS
YOU'LL
NEED:**
- [ ] newspapers
- [ ] letter patterns from pages 120-122 of this book
- [ ] shelf paper
- [ ] stapler, staples
- [ ] index cards

**Optional:**
- [ ] clothesline and clothespins

To help kids learn how to pray, try one of the following bulletin board ideas.

### Prayer Targets

Clip newspaper photos and headlines of important stories and people. Start in one corner of a bulletin board and add to the board throughout the quarter. Let the kids add their own clippings and pictures until the board is covered. Title the board "Prayer Targets." Talk about the people and events with your students. Then add the people in the news to the people in your class prayers each week. Use the board to relate Bible truths to life today.

### Prayer Hot Line

Set up a Prayer Hot Line. On index cards you and the kids list people who need class prayers. Include yourselves, family members, friends, neighbors, other church members. Add a sentence to each card describing the need. Use tacks to post the cards on a bulletin board. Or stretch clothesline across the room and clip up the cards with clothespins. Each week, each kid can take down a card and pray for that person in a class chain prayer. Or, let the kids take the cards home for the week of prayer. Remind everyone to bring the cards back the following week. When prayers are answered, be sure to note the answers on the cards and put these on another line or part of the board marked "ANSWERED." ■

# 'PSALM 150' BULLETIN BOARD

Have children put up a bulletin board to praise God for many good gifts.

Have kids cover the board with shelf paper. Then cut out construction paper letters using the patterns in this book. The title of the board should be: "Let's Praise God!"

Explain that kids will need to take snapshots of various places and people to complete the board. There may not be enough space for all categories listed below, so select several.

If cameras are not available, kids can draw pictures of these things. When pictures are finished, display them on the board.

Ask someone who prints neatly to print the following from Psalm 150. ■

## THINGS YOU'LL NEED:

- [ ] camera, film
- [ ] shelf paper
- [ ] letter patterns from pages 120-122 of this book
- [ ] stapler/tape

**LET'S PRAISE GOD!**

**Praise the Lord!**

**Praise God in . . .** (Pictures of church, school, stores, streets in your town.)

**Praise God for . . .** (Pictures of kids' pets.)

**Praise God for . . .** (Pictures of kids involved in sports.)

**Praise God for . . .** (Pictures of people in your church.)

**Praise God as you . . .** (Pictures of families doing things together.)

**Let everything that lives praise the Lord! Praise the Lord!**